The Mystery Fancier

$3

March/April·1984

The Mystery Fancier

Volume 8, Number 2
March/April 1984

TABLE OF CONTENTS

MYSTERIOUSLY SPEAKING	Page 1
The Morals of Parker By Frank D. McSherry, Jr.	Page 2
Violence and Gunplay in Crime Fiction By Robert E. Skinner	Page 9
A Report from Scandinavia By K. Arne Blom	Page 14
IT'S ABOUT CRIME By Marvin Lachman	Page 21
REEL MURDERS Movie Reviews by Walter Albert	Page 26
VERDICTS Book Reviews	Page 29
THE DOCUMENTS IN THE CASE Letters	Page 42

The Mystery Fancier
(USPS:428-590)

Steven A. Stilwell, Editor
3004 E. 25th Street
Minneapolis, MN 55406

Guy M. Townsend, Publisher
(and Eminence Grise)
1711 Clifty Drive
Madison, IN 47250

SUBSCRIPTION RATES: Second-class mail, U.S. and Canada, $15.00 per year (6 issues); first-class mail, U.S. and Canada, $18.00; overseas surfact mail, $15.00; overseas air mail, $21.00. Overseas subscribers please pay in international money order, check drawn on U.S. bank, or currency; no checks drawn on foreign banks, please. Direct correspondence and manuscripts to the editor; subscription payments and problems should be directed to the publisher.

Single copy price: $3.00
Second-class postage paid at Madison, Indiana
Copyright 1984 by Guy M. Townsend
All rights reserved for contributors
ISSN:0146-3160

Covers by Brad W. Foster

First off, here's some information on everybody's favorite convention, the Bouchercon. It will be held the weekend of October 26, 27, and 28 in the windy city of Chicago, at the Americana-Congress Hotel. The Guest of Honor, and a well-deserved honor it is, is Bill Pronzini. And, in a tradition started at the Milwaukee Bouchercon with Allen J. Hubin, the fan Guest of Honor is our own Marvin Lachman. Again, well deserved. Others scheduled to appear include: Lawrence Block, Max Collins, Stanley Ellin, William Campbell Gault, Tony Hillerman, Ed Hoch, John Lutz, Barbara Mertz, Marcia Muller, Sara Paretsky, and many, many others. For more information write: **2nd City Skulduggery, Box 576, Hinsdale, Illinois 60521.**

As advertised last time, the first issue of Bob Napier's **Mystery & Detective Monthly** is at hand. I can only say that those of you that didn't take advantage of the subscription offer are missing a sure bet. With letters from all (or at least some) of the mystery fandom elite, you can't go wrong. Support this rag. For those of you that didn't subscribe and have mislaid the information, his address is: Bob Napier, 14411-C South C Street, Tacoma, WA 98444.

A couple of personal notes. I was well satisfied with the first issue with the exception of a couple of problems, one minor and one major. First the major problem, lateness, of which this issue is also guilty. My abject apologies! How Al Hubin did **TAD** all those years and never missed a deadline is something I'll never understand. And his family still speaks to him. Oh, well. I'll try and do better and if everything goes according to plan, the next issue should follow this one in less than a month. Here's hoping.

The second problem is really only a minor annoyance. I've known the eminence grise for nearly a decade now (or maybe it only seems that long) and we've had uninterrupted correspondence over that time span and I'm here to tell you that never in all that time has he ever spelled my name wrong. So, what does he do on the masthead of the first issue under my guidance but spell my name wrong. Not my last name mind you, that I could understand, but my first name. For the record it is spelled **Steven**, not Stephen. But I'll accept contributions addressed to either one.

And speaking of contributions, we need cover art. Brad Foster has been doing wonderful work lo these many months but other commitments have precluded his doing any more save this one. So, if any of you out there are of an artistic bent or have any friends that you could dragoon, we'd sure appreciate it.

That's all for this time, but remember, it's not too early to begin planning for Chicago. I hope to see all of you there.

The Morals of Parker

Frank D. McSherry, Jr.

Parker kills.
Not for hire, as he explained once. "If I kill, it's because I don't have any choice...[because] it's only the only way to get what I want." (1)
What Parker wants is money.
But not for real. Parker is the hero (or rather, the anti-hero) of sixteen crime novels by "Richard Stark" (a pen name for Donald E. Westlake), the best series of its kind in mystery fiction. Hard and heavy, lean and mean, Parker is a professional thief, who plans large-scale operations and then sells the plans to others, more often carrying them out himself. His targets have included armored cars; Communist secret agents; a near half-million dollar payroll from a U.S. Air Force base guarded by five thousand men; and one entire medium-sized city, with its two banks, three jewelry stores, department store, loan company, and oil refinery with payroll.
He does not originate this last operation, but he approves and improves the planning. The following scene illustrates Parker's chief who seems angry at the entire community, thinks up the scheme. Using a movie projector, Edgars flashes a map of the city on a screen and, using a pointer, briefs Parker and four confederates on the plan.

> Edgar's face...showed...an excitement..."The way I thought of it," he said, "would be almost like a commando raid. Each of the five of us would captain a group of five men, including himself. Each of our groups would have specific objectives. My group would take out the police station and radio station and plant security men and telephone company building. Parker's group would go for the refinery safe, with the payroll. Paulus' group would take the Merchants' Bank..." (2)

Parker doesn't like it. For one thing, it's a waste of manpower, with four men doing nothing but stand around watching a fifth crack the bank vault; but he had more serious objections.

> "You got an operation needs an army, and the more men in a job the more chance it'll go sour. You got an operation set up by an amateur, for personal reasons...personal reasons are no good in a job because they get in the way of clear thinking." (3)

Worse, the city is located in a canyon, with steep cliffs

surrounding it on three sides and only one way in or out: "You don't go in a box with only one exit, ever." (4) This road also runs past a state police barracks; what will the cops think if they see four carloads of hard-looking strangers driving past them into town on the morning the refinery payroll arrives?

Perhaps worst of all, Edgars has been so obsessed with hurting the town, Canyon City, that he has given little thought to the getaway afterwards.

But Parker will buy it, with a few changes. Cut the number of men down from twenty-five to five; use Army walkie-talkies for communication between team units; "...we've got maybe an hour after the alarm's out. You find us a place fifty miles away or less, that we can get to without being noticed and without leaving tracks, and that the law wouldn't come in after us." (5)

When the operation begins, it climaxes in four murders, three huge fires in the city and a total take of $294,660. Parker regrets the killings, not because he he feels murder is wrong, or evil, but for professsional reasons: "...it was never good to cut down a citizen in a robbery. There's trouble enough from the law if they're just after you for a payroll, but if they're after you for Murder One you're in big trouble." (6)

This is typical of Parker's attitude to the job: nothing must be allowed to interfere with it. The job comes first. His thinking is further illustrated by an incident on another operation. Secretly, U.S. Government agents ask Parker to destroy an entire island and its immensely profitable gambling casino and tourist resort, purchased with stolen gold by a wanted Nazi war criminal they cannot touch since the island is in Cuban waters. Raze it to the ground, burn, destroy—leave nothing but scorched and smoking rock. Anything Parker gets from the robbery of the casino is his; the government will secretly provide guns, boats, other equipment, expenses, and tactfully look the other way.

Parker gets a team and sets up the operation. At the last moment, one of the team, a young lady, tells him she has a teeny-weeny problem she hasn't told him about before—she is terrified of water.

> "If this boat sinks or anything, you won't leave me, will you? You'll help me get to shore."
> If the boat sank, Parker knew this girl would be hysterical and would drown with her anyone she could get her hands on. If the boat sank, Parker would get as far from her as he could as fast as possible. But he said, "I'll help you. Don't worry about it." (7)

Parker is just as ruthless in actual practice. During the mass robbery at Canyon City, Grofield, one of Parker's lieutenants, is strongly attracted to one of the hostages, a pretty girl working as night operator at the telephone building. The attraction is mutual and intense; the girl begs Grofield to take her with him when the team leaves. Grofield does.

Parker and the others cannot understand why Grofield, a professional, has done something so impossibly stupid. By now, the girl has seen them without their masks, knows their names, is the only person who could tell the law who did the job.

The only **living** person.

Parker takes Grofield to a cliff behind their hideout at night and explains what must be done.

He stopped near the edge and said, "You can bury her down here someplace."

"Forget it, Parker. You don't kill that girl."

"That's right, I don't. She's your responsibility." (8)

"In a day or two, she'll want to home...When she tells you...she'll never tell anybody where we are or what we look like or what our names are, that's when you take care of her..."

"None of this is necessary, Parker, honest to Christ."

"Shut up...you know how to keep the law off your tail. She doesn't. They'll pick her up for jaywalking...and she'll be so rattled she'll spill the whole works." (9)

Parker talks to her, realizes she knew all along that in joining the team she was in danger of being murdered, that she knows Parker is making up his mind now whether to kill her or not. She wants adventure, excitement, luxurious living and travel; all that Canyon City has ever offered or ever will is working a telephone switchboard till retirement, listening to the thrilling sound of cucumbers growing. Grofield was her ticket out and she seized it, calmly and deliberately taking a calculated risk.

She's cooler and more sensible than Grofield in many ways, an asset to the group rather than a danger; Parker decides to let her live. She knows that too and thanks him quietly.

In **The Jugger** (1965), a teenage boy is not so fortunate. The teenager has been snooping around the house of a former, retired partner of Parker's, hoping to find hidden loot from their many robberies. By accident he finds information that will destroy Parker's current cover identity and lead to his arrest on an ald murder charge. Parker kills the boy with two blows of his big hands and buries the body in the cellar.

Well, when you go around doing things like that, killing and stealing, you've got to expect that people will badmouth you. Look at what the critics say about Parker. Anthony Boucher, the kindest and most gentle of critics, called Parker a man totally lacking in morals at all, amoral in fact, "Nobody," he said in his **New York Times Book Review** column, "tops Stark in his objective portrayal of a world of total amorality." (10) Allen J. Hubin, the respected founder and long-time editor of **The Armchair Detective**, calls him a "non-hero; the ruthless, unrepentant, single-minded operator in a humorless and amoral world..."(10a) A **Toledo Blade** reviewer calls him "a cold and skilled professional criminal."(10b) Westlake himself calls Parker "unfeeling, emotionless."(10c)

Such comments would seem decisive, especially when coming from the character's creator. Who would know better than he what his character believes and wants and is?

And yet--some of the evidence does not seem to support this conclusion. Some of it suggests that parker does indeed have a system of morality, and a familiar one at that. it just hasn't been recognized as such. Something--something--about that scene with the girl is familiar--tugs at the memory...

In **The Mourner**, (1963), Parker and his long time comrade in crime, Handy McKay, get a double job. One, steal a statue of a monk, weeping for the sins of the world, whose owner is unaware that it is a very valuable, hitherto unrecognized work by a major artist. Two, the statue's owner, attached to the diplomatic staff of an Iron Curtain Embassy here, is really a Communist secret agent. For years he has been ripping off his own government. When he is offered a stolen U.S. government document for a thousand dollars, he informs his own government that the price is one thousand five hundred and pockets the difference. The method is simple and almost undetectable; by now he has stolen almost a hundred thousand dollars and his government sends a fat, political policeman named Menlo to get it back. Legal methods are obviously out of the question, so Menlo joins forces with Parker and McKay to steal it, promising a three-way split.

Parker and McKay are not fooled. They know that Menlo intends to take the money and run—"Do you know what my pension would be", Menlo says laughing, "were I to live to the retirement age of sixty-seven? In American money, it would be—let me see—approximately five hundred and thirty dollars a year. And yet they expected me to find this hidden cache of **one hundred thousand dollars** in American money, and **bring it back**!(11). Parker and McKay are also aware of something Menlo didn't tell them—he intends to shoot them both dead as soon as possible after they find the cash.

Though they are forewarned and forearmed, Menlo nevertheless succeeds in catching them by surprise. Both believe he won't shoot in the spy's house, in a residential area, for fear of alerting neighbors and police; they are wrong. Menlo takes the risk—leaves them both badly wounded, bleeding and unconscious.

Menlo makes only one mistake. He does not stop to make sure that Parker and McKay are dead.

By the time the Communist officials arrive, Parker has regained consciousness. Fighting the pain, fighting to stay awake, Parker makes a deal with the Communists: don't call the cops, get us to a Commie doctor, hide us and heal us, and we'll get Menlo for you. No danger of an international incident that way, and no charge.

Parker adds one catch: if McKay dies, the deal is off.

And isn't that an odd thing for a man with no moral principles to say? Parker doesn't need McKay for the job; he's quite capable of doing the job alone or with another partner if he wishes. And if the deal is off, it's the cops and that old murder charge for Parker. Why would he go to such lengths to save McKay? They're old friends and co-workers in crime, yes, but not **that** close.

Parker demonstrates this surprising loyalty to the people he works with at infrequent intervals again, in **The Handle**, (1966). At the climax of Parker's raid on his island, the Nazi realizes he is losing and flees by cabin cruiser at night, leaving the island in flames behind him. The Nazi manages to reach a desolate part of the Mexican coast before the cruiser's tanks run dry, and flees into the desert carrying two heavy suitcases full of diamonds and cash.

Parker and a government agent pursue by helicopter, finding Grofield lying in the sand, badly wounded and almost unconscious. He has been shot five times; four of the wounds are trivial if painful, but the fifth, high up in the chest area, is serious.

Parker goes to a lot of trouble to help Grofield, getting the government agent to believe the wounds are not serious enough for hospitalization (which will lead the police being notified and later to a fifteen-to-twenty year sentence in a Mexican jail), later removing the agent and Mexican driver from their jeep with the aid of a monkey wrench; and finally driving Grofield at full speed to the nearest doctor.

Parker is a fast and fluent liar, as skilled with a lie as with a gun; he keeps the doctor from informing the police with a tale neatly planned to fit the Latin American temperament: "An affair of honor, senor...her husband came home unexpectedly...Yes, I know I should have brought him to a doctor two days ago, but he refused...it would mean the destruction of the reputation of the lovely lady he adores...what could I do? I appeal to you, senor, as a man of the world..."

In only one way does Parker run true to his reputed form. Though Grofield is near death and every minute counts in reaching a doctor, Parker stops, albeit briefly, to pick up the cash-loaded suitcases of the Nazi, lying abandoned by the road.

A few days later, when Grofield is awake and on the road to recovery, Parker visits him to say goodby and give him his share of the loot from the suitcases—more than $64,000.

>   Grofield said, "I appreciate this."
>   "Appreciate what?"
>   "You didn't leave me up there. You carried me along, got me my share."
>   Parker didn't understand what there was to appreciate about that. "We were working together," he said.(12)

Would a cold-hearted, amoral man have gone to such trouble, run such personal risk, when he could have been $64,000 richer by simply dumping the badly wounded man out of his jeep and leaving him to die?

Also, Parker's inability to see anything unusual in what he did in saving Grofield's life and share of the profits—you can almost hear the surprise in his remark: "we were working together!"—itself suggests that Parker has some kind of code, or ethics or morals, by which his actions weremerely standard operating procedure. It suggests that the unusual thing, the surprising thing, would have been if he'd done anything else.

And yet he risked the life he was trying so hard to save by stopping to find and pick up the suitcases packed with cash, the goal of the exercise, another indication that for Parker the job is of overriding importance, more important than life, more important than mercy or loyalty.

Critics see Parker as a man who feels nothing, except, perhaps, sullen anger, lust, and a morose desire for revenge. His own creator calls Parker "the most emotionless character I could find."(13)

Yet there is some strong evidence contradicting this conclusion. In **Deadly Edge** (1971), Parker discovers that the members of his latest team, dispersed after their latest, small-scale robbery, are being tortured and murdered one afetr the other. Security has been broken; someone, somehow, has gotten their addresses.

From Minnesota, where he made the discovery in a bloodsoaked, lonely farmhouse, Parker quickly phones Claire Carroll, the young lady he's been living with for the past three years in New York State. She's just bought a house there--Parker doesn't care for it, it's hard to defend, too many windows, too many doors; but she likes it, it's a big thing to her, their first house; so he puts up with it.

Parker warns her of the danger and tells her to get out, now, and head for a New York hotel before the killers, who've had a had start on him of some hours, show up.

To his surprise she refuses.

Claire is attracted to hard, dangerous men who lead lives of violence, but these are the kind who leave without warning and don't return; the house represents the only real security in her life.

"I picked this house with you in mind," she tells

him, "and I didn't know if you'd ever see it...someday you'll go off and you will never come back and how will I know when to stop waiting? (15) ...I know you're worried about me. But you just don't know what this house means to me...I just got into it. I won't be **driven** from it." (16)

To Parker this is not only bad tactics, it is sheer foolishness. A house is just a house, what difference does it make? But he does understand what this house—this **home**—means to Claire. She means it when she says she won't go. Instead of trying to bully her or force out or deliberately abandoning her, Parker quietly does what he can to protect her. He tells her to take all of his stuff out of the house, tell anyone who asks that she is just a message center, taking phone calls and relaying information whenever he happens to call in—and then he heads for the nearest airport.

When he phones her halfway there, between flights, certain code words and the change in her voice tells him the killers are already in the house.

Parker goes on—even though he knows the killers are armed, dangerous, and waiting for him....

Would an unfeeling man risk his life for a woman's wmotional need for a house that means nothing to him but everything to her?

How are these contradictions to be explained?

We have seen throughout Parker's insistence that the job comes first, before everything, before ordinary morality, mercy, or even the lives of his men. Perhaps we can understand Parker's system of morals better if we call the "job" by another, more precise name: not the job, but The Mission. The military mission.

The resemblance between Parker's criminal operations and military operations is striking. In the "commando raid" on Canyon City, there's the briefing, complete with maps, drawings, movie projector and pointer; the detailed staff analysis; the military terminology--"your objective is to take out the communications center"--the command structure, codes, even the use if surplus Army walkie-talkies for command and coordination.

We can now understand what Parker's questioning of Grofield's girl, after the Canyon City operation, reminds the reader of; it's a field court-martial.

The morals of Parker are the morals of a regular army man, a professional soldier, in enemy country in time of war.

Of course the job--the mission--comes first. Storm the beaches of Normandy, take the bridge at Remagen, win the war! The beaches, the bridge, victory! comes first, the lives of your men, even your closest friends, come second. You can't stop to aid a drowning friend; you have more important objectives. You dislike killing citizens, those not in uniform, every professional soldier does. And of course you do everything you cna to aid your men, once the battle is over or you're out of it; they're your comrades-in-arms. No wonder Parker was surprised at any suggestion that he should have done anything else: "We were working together" means "We're on the same side, soldier". And being a damn good company commander of combat infantry doesn't necessarily mean a lack of appreciation of the deep emotional needs of others, including the woman in your life.

Parker is a born professional soldier, a regular army man to the core. But this time the enemy isn't Nazi Germany, or North Korea, or the Viet Cong; the enemy is us.

In Parker, author Donald E. Westlake has drawn a consistent and believable portrait, (more consistent, perhaps, judging from some of comments, then he consciously realizes). And perhaps, too, this series of novels, the best series of their kind in all mystery fiction, may be trying to tell us something by such a characterization. Perhaps I am attributing to Westlake a conception that never, even unconsciously, crossed his mind. But could it that what this series—this characterization of Parker—is telling us is that there is no difference, no difference whatever, **literally** no difference—between war and crime? That what explains the one explains the other; that both have the same identical, underlying, fundamental nature? If this is true, think what a difference it would make to our views of history and politics and the world today.

After all, it isn't only Parker.

Governments kill too. For real.

NOTES

1. Stark, Richard. **The Score**. Pocket Books, 1964, p. .135.
2. Ibid. pp. 17-18.
3. Ibid. p. 13.
4. Ibid. p. 15.
5. Ibid. p. 20.
6. Ibid. p. 129.
7. Stark. **The Handle**. Pocket Books, 1966, p. 25.
8. **The Score**, op. cit. p. 130.
9. Ibid., pp. 130-131.
10. Boucher, Anthony. Quoted on the back cover of **The Rare Coin Score**. Gold Medal, 1967.
10a. Hubin, Allen J. Quoted on the back cover of the dust jacket of **Deadly Edge**. Random House, 1971.
10b. Anonymous. Quoted on the back cover of the dsut jacket of **Deadly Edge**.
10c. Westlake, Donald E. Quoted in "Interview: Donald Westlake," in "Mystery Newsletter", a department in **Ellery Queen's Mystery Magazine**, November 1976, p. 92.
11. Stark, Richard. **The Mourner**. Pocket Books, 1963, p. 64.
12. **The Handle**. op. cit., p.158.
13. Westlake., op. cit.
14. **Deadly Edge**., op. cit., p. 72.
15. Ibid. p. 63.
16. Ibid. p. 72.

Violence and Gunplay in Crime Fiction: From the Ridiculous to the Horrible

Robert E. Skinner

> I have always held, too, that pistol practice should distinctly be an open-air pastime; and when Holmes in one of his queer humours would sit in an arm-chair, with his hair-trigger and a hundred Boxer cartridges, and proceed to adorn the opposite wall with a patriotic V.R. done in bullet-pocks, I felt strongly that neither the atmosphere nor the appearance of our room was improved by it. (Dr. Watson in "The Musgrave Ritual")

> McCloor shot him three times. The bullets knocked Wales down on the sofa, back against the wall. Wales's eys popped open, bulging. His lips crawled back over his teeth, leaving them naked to the gums. His tongue came out. Then his head fell down and he didn't move any more. (The Continental Op in "Fly Paper")

The crime story has been, since its earliest days, a story concerned with violence in one form or another. Even in stories where the initial crime was not a murder (and these are rare), the criminal in them is usually moved to violence in order to cover up his transgressions. The protagonist in these stories often resorts to violence for many reasons. It may be for the protection of another character or himself. In other cases it may be simply to subdue the criminal or to exact revenge.

There has been an evolution in fictional violence that has seldom been discussed. Violence in the crime story is very important, but many practitioners of the art have handled it very haphazardly and, at times, very badly. The believability of fictional violence varies greatly from author to author, but, as we shall see here, realism is not strictly limited to more recent authors.

Though we do not necessarily associate him with this subject, Sir Arthur Conan Doyle was possibly the first crime writer to make extensive use of violence and brutality in his stories to help move the action. Though we tend to think of the Holmes stories as pleasant Victorian vignettes of crime solved through rationality and brainpower, so much violence takes place in the collection that some years ago Bruce Dettman was able to compile a book entitled **A Compendium of Canonical Weaponry** (Luther Norris, 1969). This little-known publication lists thirty-one pages of weapons, both commonplace and extraordinary, that are used to perpetrate 263 violent deaths in Doyle's Holmesian saga.

It seems to be typical of this early period that the Holmes

stories are peppered both with technical inaccuracies and sheer improbabilities. When Holmes, whom Watson has led us to believe is a crack shot, actually brings his guns into play, his actions often border on the ridiculous. The best example is seen in the climactic confrontation in **The Hound of the Baskervilles**:

> I was in time to see the beast spring upon its victim, hurl him to the ground and worry at his throat. But the next instant Holmes had emptied five barrels of his revolver into the creatures flank.

Even a novice must ask how Holmes could successfully dispatch the "horrible hound" by shooting off his backside. As a doctor, Doyle should have been ashamed.

On the other side of the coin, Doyle could produce a reasonably believable violent confrontation, as in "The Adventure of Charles Augustus Milverton". As Holmes and Watson watch from their hiding place, they witness Milverton's fate as he receives one of his victims:

> "You will ruin no more lives as you have ruined mine. You will wring no more hearts as you wrung mine. I will free the world of a poisonous thing. Take that you hound, and that!--and that!--and that!--and that!--and that!"
>
> She had emptied barrel after barrel into Milverton's body, the muzzle within two feet of his shirt front. He shrank away and then fell forward upon the table, coughing furiously and clawing among the papers. then he staggered to his feet, received another shot and rolled upon the floor.
>
> "You've done me", he cried, and lay still. The woman looked at him intently and ground her heel into his upturned face.

Of all the scenes Doyle wrote, few have the shocking, brutal power of this image of a high-born, aristocratic woman reduced to the level of a cold-blooded murderer. The image of the heel being ground into Milverton's dying face tends to drive away even the silliness of the melodramatic dialog.

As the twentieth century turned, violence became an accepted feature of crime and adventure novels, though it did not necessarily become more believable. Very little blood was actually spilled when a scene called for it and the reader often had to wade through a lot of melodramatic dialog or narration that was used to tell him how horrible the scene was, rather than describe how it must have been.

Another important aspect of this form of writing was the fact that there could be no ambiguity between the hero and the villain. The hero could not commit an act of violence unless he was pushed into it. Some of the best examples of this unwritten code can be seen in the little known **Norroy, Diplomatic Agent** by Charles Bronson Howard (Saalfield, 1907). in this pre-James Bond espionage thriller, the hero finds himself, ironically enough, pitted against Russian secret police, and is forced to flee:

> They were out of the city now, and were nearing the railroad station. If his horse could only hold out until he reached the hills! His pursuer fired and a bullet whistled through Norroy's felt hat.

> Norry knew that he could do but one thing. His horse was stumbling and could carry him but a few paces further. Suddenly he swerved him from his path, turned him squarely in the Russian's way, and jerked him to a standstill. With his free hand, he aimed at the oncoming pursuer, and the shot caught the Russian fairly in the center of the forehead. The man quietly collapsed and tumbled from his horse. (p. 279)

This code of "letting the other man draw first" seems to have been familiar to both Americans and Britons, because we see it exemplified by many heroes during the Edwardian period, particularly those of Louis Joseph Vance and Sax Rohmer. This tendency to be a gentleman, no matter what the provocation, occurs over and over again. The enemy is always given another chance to behave and admit defeat, but he never takes it:

> The Russian took the desired articles from his pocket and held them out to Norroy. The secret agent stretched forth his hand. The Russian gripped it tightly and his other hand shot forth and seized the wrist of the one holding the dagger. With a sudden motion of his body Norroy twisted back both of his opponent's hands; then, wheeling quickly, caught him about the neck in such a way as to render him powerless.
> "Madame," Norroy said, dispassionately, "your property is on the floor. I must ask you to pick it up." As the Countess Helma moved forward, he spoke in a very low tone to the man in his embrace. "If you attempt that again, Captain Lenoff, you will have your dirk restored to you in a way you won't like...Haven't you enough wits to see that I have the upper hand?" (pp. 298-9)

Of course, the time for this gentlemenly style had just about run out. By the early 1920s, an entirely new style of crime fiction was beginning to appear, particularly in the pulp magazines. Well-bred heroes like Norroy, Maxwell Sanderson, Nayland-Smith, and Raffles had no place in this hard-boiled world. Nowhere was this new world better depicted than between the garish covers of **Black Mask**. As envisioned by editors Phil Cody and Captain Joseph T. Shaw, the **Black Mask** milieu was one inhabited by crooked politicians, racketeers, and killers. Gentleman-adventurers and amateurs couldn't hope to contend with this gang. It was going to take someone who played dirty and scorned the rules.

The first and foremost of this new breed of crime hero was Carroll John Daly's Race Williams. Williams was the essence of the western cowpoke set down in modern-day New York City. He worked alone and expressed contempt for official police and agency dicks alike. Williams had no use for ratiocination and deduction; his style was to lower his head and go in swinging. he always carried at least two Colt .44 specials and there is ample evidence that he enjoyed using them:

> The papers were always either roasting me for shooting down some minor criminals or praising me for gunning out the big shots. But when you're hunting the top guy, you have to kick aside--or shoot aside--the

gunmen he hires. You can't make hamburger without grinding up a little meat.

It is interesting to note that the impact in a typical Race Williams story comes, not from the author's own depiction of smashed faces or spurting arteries, but rather from the fiendish, brutal pleasure that Williams gets from inflicting damage on his enemies:

> ...I looked right down the blue barrel of a German Luger. Hard, red knuckles showed white. And--I shot him five times. Five times, smack in the stomach, before he could even squeeze the trigger. Surprised? He was amazed. At least, he should have been. Anyway he was dead--deader then hell before he folded up and sat down on the floor. (**Murder from the East**, p.10

There is an intentional irony in some of Williams' dialog as in this scene after he pistol-whips an enemy into unconsciousness for the second time in the same day:

> I stood for a minute looking down at him. Generally when I slap a guy down he doesn't bob up again two or three minutes later. But this guy! I looked at the bandage around his head, hesitated a momnet, then cracked him again. It wasn't pleasant, neither for him nor for me. But I couldn't let my highmindedness be the cause of the brutal murder of a child. (**Murder from the East** p.71)

Of all of Race's qualities, his highmindedness is the one that we need least be concerned about. His stories are those of a schoolyard bully, and his depiction of his own adventures has the self-conscious ring of a child justifying his pulling the wings off butterflies.

While Daly's stories provided a prototype for the new "hard-boiled school", the better writers steered clear of his brand of melodramatic brvado. Even though violence and brutality are very much a part of this style, the more proficient practioners had a more detached way of expressing it. At times it seems almost as clinical as a laboratory dissection, as in Raymond Chandler's "Spanish Blood":

> [Delaguerra] went into the bathroom and got a glass of water and threw it into the Filipino's face as hard as he could throw it.
> Toribo jerked, gagged sharply as the wire caught his neck. His eyes jumped open. He opened his mouth to yell.
> Delaguerra jerked the wire taut against the brown throat. The yell was cut off as though by a switch. There was a strained anguished gurgle. Toribo's mouth drooled.
> Delaguerra let the wire go slack again and put his head down close to the Filipino's head. He spoke to him gently, with a dry, very deadly gentleness.
> "You want to talk to me, spig. Maybe not right away, maybe not even soon. But after awhile you want to talk to me."

Torture scenes abound in hard-boiled fiction, and sometimes they are elaborate in their brutality. The beating of Ned Beaumont goes on for pages in Dashiell Hammett's **The Glass Key**. However, the same horror could often be conveyed in a few ambivalent lines, as in:

> Carver lifted the gun and smelled it, watching him from under his brows. His lower jaw came out a little and he brought his own automatic up to Tammany's chin, breaking the flesh. The fat man wiped dazedly at the blood. (Thomas Walsh, "Best Man" 1934)

This type of writing spawned its own style of grim humor, which was as ugly in its own way as the violence it mocked. Consider this discussion between some police detectives at the end of a case that has left three men stabbed or shot to pieces in a lawyer's study:

> Prentice laughed suddenly, set his glass down. "I feel sorry for the poor guy. He's got the messiest rug I ever saw in my life." He grinned at Allen, added, "The hell he'll catch when his old lady gets home". (Roger Torrey, "Clean Sweep", 1934)

While female villains were far from new during this period, the hard-boiled femme fatale was far more dangerous than her Victorian sister who relied on sex and an occasional vial of poison. There is a real shock to the power in the way these women advanced feminine equality. In Norbert Davis's "Red Goose" (1934) a female protagonist soaks up quite a beating before the detective makes his move and changes the balance of power. However, when he isn't quite equal to the task, the woman steps in:

> Carter bounced to his feet instantly. He ran down the hall towards the stairs.
> "Carter!"
> It was Marjorie Smith. She was standing in the doorway and she had the .45 automatic...in one small hand.
> Carter whirled around like a dancer and jumped sideways crouching. Marjorie Smith shot him.
> The bullet caught Carter and slammed him back and down in a limp pile. His arms and legs moved aimlessly. After a second he got slowly to his feet and staggered down the hall.
> Marjorie Smith shot him again, deliberately, in the back. Carter collapsed weakly and slid down the stairs, bumping soddenly on each step.

A number of interesting theories have evolved concerning the public's attitude to violence in the twentieth century. One of the most interesting was set forth by Colin Watson in his landmark study **Snobbery with Violence**(1971). Watson suggests that "violence was not, in the 1920's, the psychological abstraction that has so deeply concerned social diagnosticians since the end of the second world war. Although millions had been slaughtered and millions more maimed, the survivors of the 1914-1918 war saw no relationship between the feroctiy on the battlefield and cruel behavior elsewhere....Civilians regarded (war's) horrors as a special case--deplorable, certainly, but quite separate from domestic ills".

It is true, though, that the end of World War I produced a

certain disillusionment with traditional values, a situation that was only heightened by governmental incompetence, and greed and corruption among elected officials. This situation seems to have been as true in Great Britain as it was in the United States.

Perhaps as a result of this impatience with law and older values, two particularly extraordinary heroes appeared in British fiction in the 1920s. 1920 saw the appearance of H.C. (Sapper) McNeil's **Bulldog Drummond**. Drummond was depicted as an ex-military officer who had grown so accustomed to the excitement of war that he found peacetime intolerable. To combat boredom, he surrounded himself with other like-minded young chaps and began a career of foiling the plans of international criminal masterminds, mad scientists, and anarchists.

Sapper depicts Drummond as a boyish, likable fellow with great physical strength, bulldog tenacity, and a magical charisma. We get some insight into his character when we are told in this first adventure that Drummond had made a second career in the war of crawling behind enemy lines to strangle or break the necks of German soldiers.

Much of the violence in the Drummond stories is made to seem appealing through Sapper's light-hearted way of describing it. A shooting or beating is often passed off as being "potted", being "put to sleep", or, more frequently as "a good biff". There is, however, a neofascist attitude at the heart of all these highjinks. Colin Watson has noted that Drummond has very little patience with official police forces and would not hesitate "to incapacitate any whose bumbling regard for the proprieties threatened to interfere with his right to fight". To make matters worse, Drummond's adversaries are often "unwashed foreign blokes" or "nasty little Jews", a fact that plays on the conscious or unconcious prejudices of the reader and makes the violence even more acceptable. After all, they deserve it, don't they?

The second, and even more violent, fictional hero to come out of Great Britain in the 20s was Leslie Charteris's Simon Templar. Templar, known as the Saint, is, if anything, a more fantastic character than Drummond. A headache to the law and the underworld alike, Templar and his gang engage themselves in adventures for profit as well as for fun. As "The Robin Hood of Modern Crime" it is Templar's conceit to relieve criminals of their "boodle" after they have stolen it from someone else. As boyishly lovable as Drummond, the Saint is an avowed killer who will go anywhere and do anything if the stakes are high enough. In his earlier adventures in particular, we find him doing everything from single-handedly foiling a Central American revolution to acting as the paid assassin for a vengeful New York millionaire.

Torture, gunplay, and worse abound in the average Saint story, but it is in hand-to-hand combat that Templar really shines. Many of these fights artfully mingle the gush of blood with the lyric qualities of poetry:

> The man on the Saint's right felt a stab of fire lance across the tendons of his wrist...and he heard Ualino cry out. That was about as much as anybody saw or understood. Somehow, without a struggle, the Saint was free; and a steel blade flashed in his hand. It swept upwards in front of him in a terrible arc; and Ualino clutched at his stomach and sank down, with his knees buckling under him and a ghastly crimson tide bursting between his fingers...and then the knife swept on upwards, and the hilt of it struck the electric light bulb over the table and brought utter darkness with an explosion like a

gun. (**The Saint in New York**, p.101)

By the 1940s, violence in crime fiction seems to have become somewhat toned down. It existed, of course, but much of it was understated or occurred offstage. Even heroes like the Saint, who appeared in anumber of wartime adventures, tended to rely more on guile and less on guns. In Raymond Chandler's work during this period, the emphasis was not so much on the actual violence as on the depravity of the characters. Readers often found the moral decay in his work and that of his imitators more shocking than the blood and gore of the 20's and 30's.

1949 was a kind of watershed in that it marked the appearance of Mickey Spillane's Mike Hammer. Hammer can be considered a lineal descendent of Race Williams. The verbal bullying, the speeches of self-justification, and the reliance on heavy artillery rather than deduction are all pages out of Carroll John Daly's book. In **I, The Jury**, Hammer's first outing, the reader is witness to a masterpiece of literary brutality. A thug is beaten by Hammer until his teeth come through his skin, several others are shot to death, and the climax comes when Hammer discovers that the woman he loves is both a dealer in narcotics and a killer. He unhesitatingly shoots her in the belly with a .45 as they embrace. As she asks with her dying breath how he could do it, Hammer sneers "it was easy".

This became the hallmark of Spillane's work. Women are usually depicted as extraordinarily sexy and beautiful, but they are also evil. Their evil is always so pervasive and ingrained that Hammer msust blow them to pieces in the most sickening way possible in order to exorcise them. It is interesting to note, though, that in the current television version on CBS, **Mickey Spillane's Mike Hammer**, Mike is portrayed with punctilious good-guyism by mild-mannered Stacy Keach. For all of carrying a .45 automatic under his arm, he hasn't even seriously wounded anyone with it yet. The brutal Hammer has been homogenized by televison into a New York Philip Marlowe.

In the early 1950's, the important crime writer to come on the scene was Ian Fleming with his stories of James Bond. Bond was something of a novelty duirng the peacefulness of the Eisenhower years because he was a professional killer for the British Secret Service. Other detectives may kill in the line of duty, but very seldom has a protagonist come along who could truly say that murder was his business.

But the Bond stories, while interesting, are relativley bloodless. Bond kills a number of people in various artful ways, but there is a curious bloodlessness to the killings, to be slightly facetious. Fleming started out well enough in **Casino Royale** with a torture scene to shrivel the loins of the toughest reader. Bond is captured by the villain, Le Chifre, and, after being stripped naked, is lashed to a chair which has had its cane bottom cut out of it. Then, Bond's male equippage, hanging through the bottom is lashed with some sort of cane-spiked fly swatter until he is a dreadful mess. Later, what the doctors have to do to set him right sounds almost as bad as the torture.

Many of the other killings or maimings in James Bond's canon are bizarre, in that they are mildly interesting, but few really grab our attention. For example, in **Goldfinger**, Bond's climatic fight with Oddjob ends with the gigantic oriental being sucked out the window of a high-flying jet plane. In **Live and Let Die**, Bond has his final confrontation with Ernst Stavro Vlofeld, the arch fiend who killed Bond's wife in **On Her Majesty's Secret Service**. One would have hoped that this would be the fight of the century, replete with smashed faces, bullet pocked bodies, and spurting arteries. But this was not to be. Bond and Blofeld have a bit of a faceoff; Bond armed with a sword-stick and Blofeld with a samuri sword. In a trice Bond disarms Blofeld and has him around the throat. As he hisses "die, Blofeld, die", Blofeld's tongue falls out, his eyes roll back in his head, and he obligingly expires. One who has been raised on James Bond movies and never read the books might be surprised to find how tame the books are.

Fleming did do something for the crime novel; he made sex moare acceptable. Not sordid sex, as one might find in Mickey Spillane, but nice, normal, heterosexual sex. Of course, like the violence, the sex was somewhat understated. As the 1960's turned, however, more graphic sex began to be seen in crime fiction and, perhaps in consequence, more graphic violence as well. Two writers of crime fiction who began in the 60's and are still writing today are John D. MacDonald and Donald Hamilton. Sex and violence are very much a part of each writer's output and neither pulls punches in his depiction.

MacDonald's most important creation is Travis McGee, a big, handsome, likable ex-football player. He lives on his houseboat, "The Busted Flush", and enjoys a sybaritic lifestyle with no real visible means of support. When asked, he usually answers that he's in salvage. His adventures result from his meetings with friends and acquaintances who have been bilked or flummoxed out of large sums of money. McGee offers to use his brains, brawn, and faintly larcenous soul to retrieve the lost fortunes, provided that he recieve exactly half the take. Since half is better than nothing, no one ever refuses the offer.

When McGee descends to the criminal underworld, it is a dark and dangerous place indeed. It is inhabited, not just with unscrupulous criminal types, but also with a hoard of insane, beastial persons of boht sexes who will kill, maim, and otherwise destroy for the sheer pleasure of it. This madness of McGee's opponents has become the hallmark of MacDonald's work. As their madness is slowly uncovered little by little until McGee and the reader face them in their demonic fury, the reader can actually find himself frightened by the fiendishness of MacDonald's imagination.

One of the best examples of this dark netherworld can be seen in **A Tan and Sandy Silence** (1971). McGee, tracking down a former flame whom he believes to be in trouble, meets Lisa Dissat, a ruthless and unscrupulous sexpot and tries to use her to lead him either to the missing girlfriend or to the man responsible for her disappearance. The man, Paul Dissat, Lisa's cousin, catches on and nearly kills McGee with a baseball bat. As McGee comes to on the beach, he finds himself tied up and Lisa buried up to her neck in the sand with the tide about to come in. He describes her death with a soft lyricism that fascinates as it horrifies:

> Her black hair was fanned out, and in the instant of sharpened, memorable vision I saw the spume of sand drifting out of her open mouth, like a strange cartoon balloon, a message without sound. A sandy, tan farewell. (p.191).

The fact that Lisa herself is a heartless criminal, responsible for the deaths of two people does nothing to mitigate the horror of her death.

Most of the killings seen in McGee's adventures are just as bizarre as this. People aren't just shot or stabbed, they are crushed under engine blocks, buried alive in vats of molten asphalt, impaled on shards of glass in a broken window, and suddenly blown to bits. McGee himself is responsible for many of the deaths. He takes very few people in alive to the law. But, interestingly enough, many of the deaths of his enemies are such that they are not quite his fault. They are killed in falls, run in front of speeding automobiles, or, attempting to escape, fall overboard and impale themselves on sharp bamboo.

McGee is actually a very sensitive guy for someone in such a violent profession. He kills but feels remorse. After killing a hood in a stand-up gun battle, he muses:

> It numbs, always, even when you keep asking yourself what other choice you had. Somebody watched him pull himself up by the crib bars and stand cooing and drooling, and thought him a damned fine baby.

As he buries the gunman's body in the sand, he hears himself "making small whimpering sounds" but shuts his teeth hard and cuts it off.

In spite of this sensitive streak, an aroused McGee is a terrible figure. In **The Green Ripper**, which is MacDonald's equivalent to **Red Harvest**, McGee goes undercover to track down a band of terrorists who have murdered his lover, Gretchen. After infiltrating the gang and becoming a trusted member, he exacts his revenge in a full chapter during which he shoots, stabs, bludgeons, and otherwise massacres more than a half-dozen people. He has to be psychoanalyzed after it is over, but he is damned efficient while he is about it.

McGee's exact opposite is Donald Hamilton's Matt Helm. Helm is like James Bond in that he is an assassin for a government, but he is totally unlike him in just about every other way. Helm likes his work and, at the same time, seems to be a likable, well-adjusted guy. He reasons that he is a public servant of the United States just like any other. The only exception is that he kills people.

Helm has much more in common with Dashiell Hammett's Continetal Op than with James bond. Both work for nameless bosses whose cold-blooded politeness is a source of wonder and delight to their respective employees. Each is a loyal corporation man; they are the top men in their agencies and are proud of it.

Helm works for a nameless organization that has its roots in World War II. The head of the organization, whom we know for many books only as "Mac", organized and trained an elite band of men and women in the most efficient methods of stalking and killing. Young Captain Helm came to Mac's attention because of his expertise as a hunter and a tracker and became, by war's end, one of Mac's top agents. A meeting in 1960 with a former female collegue ends Helm's retirement and comfortable married life, which he supported by writing Louis Lamour-type westerns and articles for magazines like **Field and Stream**. With his marriage in tatters and his sudden realization that he misses his old life, Helm rejoins Mac and soon, in spite of his advanced age, reclaims his title as "top gun".

Life is cheap to Helm, though he can feel remorse for the loss of a friend or lover. When Mac gives the order for him to "make the touch",however, nothing stands in his way. More than one antagonist finds this out to his sorrow. When Caselius tries to use Louise Taylor as a hostage in **The Wrecking Crew**, Helm simply aims his gun at all four legs in order to bring his man down. The fact that he actually hits Caselius and is easily able to finish him off without harming

Louise is of little consequence. When Willi Kelm tries the same trick with Bobbie Prince in **The Poisoners**, the added threat of a cocked .44 magnum in her back does not deter Matt from shooting him down.

Matt knows nothing of the remorse that Travis McGee feels at the death of an enemy. He always sees them off as they lay dying, but he sheds no tears; to him dying is part of the game, as he tells Lacy Rockwell after she has tried to kill him in **The Intimidators**:

"I'm dying, aren't I?"
"I should hope so," I said. "If not, we'll have to send my associate back to markmanship school."
After a shocked moment, she managed a little ghost of a laugh. "Thanks," she gasped. "Thanks for not feeling obliged to lie unconvincingly and tell me I'm going to be find, just fine."
"That bullshit is for amateurs," I said. "We're all pros here, aren't we?"

The most important aspect of the violence and brutality in a Matt Helm story is its ambivalence. Everything, from a soldering iron used on Matt's chest to extract information, to the delivery of a long-range pistol shot to the body are discussed with the nonchalance of a story at a cocktail party. Matt Helm is simply an ordinary joe telling you about what he does, just like any other neighbor. The horror lies in the fact that he is a killer.

Many other authors, past and present, have used violence as an integral part of their work. New authors come along all the time and it seems that the better ones working in the crime genre have learned to use it effectively by portraying it as realistically as possible. Ken Follett is an excellent example of this new breed of crime writer whose depictions of violent death are just one more level of the research used to create a realistic and dramatic story. One is inclined to wonder, though, how much further can they go?

A Report from Scandinavia

K. Arne Blom

Over here many of us have been nursing the belief that the hardboiled mystery is something that must be written by an American writer and take place in a big city, like L.A., New York, Chicago, or whatever. The main reason for this might be that the hardboiled mystery is an American invention and most efforts by European writers to write hardboiled mysteries have been so embarrassing.

Maybe different parts of the world, the different continents, each have their own special tone and melody. I mean, have you ever read a hardboiled mystery that takes place in Rio de Janeiro or a whodunit that takes place in Central Park? I claim that a book written in Spanish is very different from a book written in English, which is enormously different from a book written in German, which is nothing like a book written in Swedish. The kind of problem might be the same: a corpse is a corpse and a dead man a dead man. But the private eye is different in London as compared to San Francisco, and the police force works differently in Rome as compared to New York.

So the hardboiled way of writing and thinking and living is something that belongs to a certain continent? To a certain country? To the US of A? Yeah, I thought so until I read the first mystery by a new Danish crime writer. He is not at all a new writer—he had written at least 60 books before he tried his talent on a mystery. He was well known as a fine poet and an interesting essayist.

His name is Dan Turell, one of the finest **describers** of the wonderful city of Copehagen ever—or Kobenhavn, the city's true name. So far he has published five mysteries about a nameless free-lance journalist who happens to be dragged into cases. The amazing thing is that Dan Turell has found his own hardboiled tone and style, which is true hardboiled in the traditional way and at the same time still his own. Three of the books are taking place in Kobenhavn—and they become something of a Op Blues.

Here is something for an American publisher with a good nose for good mysteries to keep an eye on.

Frankly, there are about ten or so, maybe more, mysteries published in the Scandinavian countries that are as good—and in some cases even better—than the main part of what is being written and published in the US or England. But how many of them get a chance, how many are translated? Well, there is a basic problem, and that is money. It costs money to translate a book. Then you have to find an audience interested in reading about cases in Falun, Lund, Rickarum, Rodby and other exotic places in the world.

Over here we love to read a good mystery set in New Mexico or in Madison, Indiana, or in Mamaroneck. We love to read a good mystery. I personally am very fond of the books of Arthur Upfield. Apart from being damned good books they tell me a lot about a part of the world I know little about. There is a great educational value in a good mystery.

To come to the point: I am sure the American reading audience likes to read a good mystery because it is a good book worth reading. But the sad thing is that you are missing so many good books written over here, but never translated. I think it would help a great deal if the Mystery Writers of America were to give an Edgar for the best mystery of the year in translation.

A hope that we started to nurse when the International Crime Congresses were started in 1975 was that we would get a chance to teach the English-speaking world that there are good mysteries written in Swedish, Danish, and Norwegian. There are more than Sjowall-Wahloo and some other known ones, but it remains for the publishers to discover that they were informed about this fact when they attended the congresses in London, New York, and Stockholm.

This concludes the first report from this side of the big water. I have promised to write a piece now and then and tell a little about the mystery in Europe. So I'll be back. In the meantime, call your favorite publisher and tell him about the good Danish writer dan Turell. I won't mind if you should happen to mention my name at the same time. It was some years ago I had a book translated into English. My latest translation came out in Russia in Russian. They print 180,000 copies when they publish the first edition.

IT'S ABOUT CRIME
by Marvin Lachman

• NOTES ON RECENT READING

How does one measure a book with a $75.00 price tag? For the real mystery fan, **Crime Fiction, 1749-1980: A Comprehensive Bibliography** by Allen J. Hubin, may be one of the biggest bargains of all time. Amortized over the life of the life of the book, its cost will be pennies a day to provide its owner with an unbelievable amount of information. More than 8,600 titles have been added to the 50,000+ titles in the first edition, published in 1979. There have also been many corrections, provide by authors and students knowledgeable in the field. The most pleasant surprise is in the number of new features, especially:

1. A Settings Index in which the location of most books is given, often including the specific city. (Had this book only been available when I started my series on "The American Regional Mystery"!)

2. A Series Character Index wherein all characters who have appeared in five or more books are listed, along with the year of their first appearance, type of series, e.g. spy, private eye, et.al., and number of books in series.

The heart of the book remains an awe-inspiring author index of 438 pages in which every author is listed alphabetically as, in turn, are all of their titles. Here, too, is found information on their date of birth and death, their series characters, settings, and information as to publisher and date of publication for each book. For those who have a title in mind but don't know an author, there is also an alphabetical title index of 190 pages.

"Indispensable" is not a word I toss around lightly, but it is the only one which fits this monumental work, published by Garland.

A more specialized reference work, but one which is invaluable to readers of espionage fiction, is Andy East's **The Cold War File**, Scarecrow Press, $22.50. Eighty authors are covered, and East includes considerable biographical information not only about the authors, but also about their series characters. There is also complete bibliographical data about each book in the various series and a very helpful secret agent index at the end. east's knowledge of the field is encyclopedic. covering even the marketing strategies under which many of the series were publicized and sold. Let's hope this book never falls into Russian hands; considering the ineptness of the CIA, it may be our most valuable weapon in the Cold War.

Even more specialized is a reference work limited to a single author, **The Agatha Christie Companion: The Complete Guide to Agatha Christie's Life and Work** by Dennis Sanders and Lou Lovallo, from

Delacorte Press at $19.95. Considering the author, her fame, quality, and longevity, she is worth an entire reference book.

Not that this is the first such book about Christie. The authors list eleven previous works in their bibliography, but omit at least two others. But their's is the best of the lot in many respects. Events in Christie's life are well related to the books she was working on at the time. And though other books have given plot summaries, these are the best. They will help readers relive their reading of Christie's works. This book is especially good on the adaptations of Christie to stage, screen, and television, providing many up-to-date details, including complete cast listings.

Christie wrote 95 books that have sold more than 500 million copies and provide countless hours of enjoyment to her readers. It is only fitting that she be the subject of a reference work so large (524 pages), so well-done, and so useful. It helps repay the debt we all owe to the "Queen of Mystery".

Hail to thee, Southern Illinois University! Not only did you produce Walt Frazier who led the New York Knicks to two NBA championships, you have now produced two championship short story collections. The first is **Exeunt Murderers, The Best Mystery Stories of Anthony Boucher**, edited by Francis M. Nevins and Martin Greenberg. There is also a ten page introduction by Nevins that is merely perfect. Who can resist reading a collection which, quite accurately, opens with the following first paragraph as its introduction:

> An Anthony Boucher walks the earth but once. he treated every day of his adult life as the bountiful universe's invitation to create, to enjoy and help others enjoy creations, to care. Whatever he touched he made come alive with his informed love. He excelled at all he did, and the things he did best no one will ever do better.

In addition to his superb introduction Nevins also provides a complete checklist to Boucher's mysteries and science fiction.

There are 23 mysteries in this collection, and there are some beauties among them. Nine feature Nick Noble, the previously uncollected ex-policeman, who solves his cases without ever visiting the crime scene. "QL 696.C9", "Crime Must Have a Stop", and, "The Girl Who Married a Monster" are especially good. Even better is "The Stripper", one of two stories about Boucher's nun-detective, Sister Ursula. Of the non-series stories, "Threnody" and "The Statement of Jerry Malloy" are ny favorites, but there isn't a bad story in the book.

Boucher was that cliche, "a Renaissance Man". His broad learning and wit is reflected as clearly in these tales as it was in his incomparable reviews for the **The New York Times Book Review**. He loved the pure detective story, and his intricate plotting, even under the difficulties of the short story length, demonstrates this time and again.

Also available at the same price from the same publisher is a second volume in the "Mystery Makers" series. It is **Buffet for Unwelcome Guests: The Best Short Mystery Short Stories of Christianna Brand**. The editors are the same, but this time the introduction, equally well-written and knowledgeable, is by Robert E. Briney.

Not yet a household name in this country (though she deserves to be), Brand is a legend to those who have heard her delightful tales at gatherings of mystery fans. Her wit and intelligence come across when she speaks and also when she writes. **Buffet**, which, like the

Boucher book, is about 300 pages, contains 16 stories, many of which are new to U.S. readers. I suspect that sixteen readers, if asked, would have sixteen different stories. My choice is "Poison in the Cup", one òf four stories about her series sleuth, Inspector Cockrill. As a hint for those who don't remember the name, he was the detective (played so well by Alistair Sim) in the superb film version of Brand's most famous novel, **Green for Danger.**

And, of course, there's a checklist here, too, so that the reader that logically wants to go beyond these stories can trace the complete works of Christianna Brand.

Another university publisher doing interesting things in the mystery field is the University of Pittsburgh Press. They have a Descriptive Bibliography series of outstanding American authors which includes the following in our genre:

1. **Dashiell Hammett** by Richard Layman, 185 pp. $17.50
2. **Raymond Chandler** by Matthew Bruccoli, 146 pp. $23.00
3. **Ross Macdonald** by Matthew Bruccoli, 259 pp. $40.00

All three are in a uniform, extremely attractive format which includes publishing information about the complete works of each writer. This provides some deliciously obscure information about their early appearances in print.

Also included is detailed publishing information about all of their mysteries, hardcover and paperback. (Each had at least one book that was first published in paper covers.) There are illustrations of the title page and covers for every book. These pictures not only provide information, but seeing how a book **looked** when first published helps the reader to place it into the context of its time. Bibliographies of these three famous hard-boiled writers have been done before, but none even approached these for completeness, appearance, and accuracy. I hope the prices won't be prohibitive for mystery fans who do not go around disguised as well endowed libraries.

Two unusually lively, well-illustrated biographies have recently come my way. **Improbably Fiction: The Life of Mary Roberts Rinehart** by Jan Cohn, 293 pages at $16.95, also comes from the University of Pittsburgh, and while originally published in 1980, is still in print. Cohn is very knowledgeable about Rinehart's writing, both mystery and non-mystery and includes a chronological bibliography. She does an excellent job of telling the fascinating life of this woman who had so many careers: nurse, fiction- writer, foreign correspondent, publisher, wife and mother, etc. Rinehart has been dead for more than 25 years, and it is easy to forget how popular she once was. Jan Cohn reminds us and helps us document the Rinehart success by telling the prices she was paid for her published works.

Except that both were extremely prolific writers, it is hard to find two people less alike than Rinehart and Georges Simenon. The latter is the subject of **The Mystery of Georges Simenon** by Fenton Bresler, published at $16.95 from Beaufort Books. Considering the publicity that has been given to Simenon's alleged prodigious sexual feats, it is not surprising that Bresler gives far more attention to Simenon's personal life than to his writing. Not to worry; the detailed analysis of the Maigret canon is yet to be written. Meanwhile, be thankful for an eminently readable biography of a very interesting and controversial writer.

There is much in the best-seller **Coroner** by Thomas T. Noguchi, M.D., with Joseph Di Mona, that will appeal to fans of such fictional sleuths of the past as Dr. Thorndyke and Craig Kennedy. Without being overburdened with technical detail, the reader receives an overview of the history and practice of forensic medicine. Anyone who shares with

me awe at the "miracles" which science can accomplish in crime detection will be fascinated by this book.
Yet I suspect that the book's popularity stems from the notoriety Dr. Noguchi has received in his battles with the Los Angeles government and the fame of some of the victims whose deaths he investigated. He personally did the autopsies on Marilyn Monroe, Robert F. Kennedy, and Sharon Tate; he was responsible for those conducted on Janis Joplin, William Holden, Natalie Wood, and John Belushi. If Noguchi's book is self-serving and hurriedly written, it is also extremely readable. It will permit readers to get many of the facts regarding the cases which were (and still are) distorted every week by the rags sold at the checkout counters of our local markets.

I have often said that in the field of international espionage truth is more fascinating than anything the imagination can devise. Witness the theory advanced by Claire Sterling in **The Time of the Assassins**, from Holt, Rinehart, and Winston at $14.95. Which is the Russian KGB, operating through the Bulgarian secret service, was responsible for the 1981 assassination attempt on Pope John Paul II. When that idea was first advanced, many scoffed because the assassin, Hehmed Ali Agca, was apparently a member of a right-wing terrorist group and had been in a Turkish prison for murdering a liberal newspaper editor. Yet, how did he succeed in escaping, spending 50 days in Sofia, having enough money to travel in luxury throughout Europe before trying to kill the Pope?

Perhaps Mrs. Sterling has convinced me because I'm willing to believe the worst about extremists of Right and Left. The same lack of morality which led to the Soviet-Nazi pact in 1940 is still operative. The likely motive: to teach a lesson to a Polish Pope who had supported the Solidarity movement. I have no trouble seeing Bulgaria making a successful appeal to the fanaticism, ego, and selfishness of Agca. The Bulgarian government is one of the most amoral around, trafficking in drugs and sending assassins abroad to murder exiles with poisoned umbrella tips. Top that idea, John Le Carre!

Claire Sterling (her husband, Thomas, has written four mystery novels) generates considerable suspense as she relates her efforts to dig up facts on the case; she enters it as an expert on world terrorism. She tends to be repetitious and there are holes in her thesis which I suspect will cause those less ready to be convinced to be dubious. I also wish she had spent more time telling us what made Agca tick, but perhaps that is the subject for another book.

Notes on Recent Viewing

Showtime, the cable TV network, did an adaptation of a **A Talent for Murder**, the Edward Chodorov-Norman Panama play which won an Edgar in 1982. I did not see the original play which starred Claudette Colbert and Jean-Pierre Aumont, but the television cast was equally impressive, with Angela Lansbury and Laurence Olivier, though one had the feeling that the latter was merely walking through his lines.

Lansbury, on the other hand, was excellent even if she reminded me too much of Bette Davis. She plays a wealthy, aging mystery writer who is addicted to booze, cigarettes, and computer gimmickry. Her avaricious family comes to celebrate her birthday and possibly to do her in before she can change her will or otherwise dispose of her property, which includes Picasso originals. Reminiscent of other stage thrillers like **Deathtrap** and **Sleuth** because of its twists and surprises, it was not nearly as good. The plotting was not as tight, nor the dialogue as sophisticated. Still, **A Talent for Murder** was fun and, for the devotee of what Ira Levin calls "Thrilleritis Malignis", worth spending an hour and a half with.

The highly publicized return of Mickey Spillane's Mike Hammer to network TV was a total washout as far as I was concerned. They scheduled a two hour film for a Thursday night 9 to 11 P.M. Since that conflicted with **Hill Street Blues**, hammer lost out. On the following Saturday the regular premire took place, and I should have missed that, too. I didn't expect a great plot, but the poor imitation of one was too much to endure. It was a mish-mash of drugs, show business, gold scams, and terrorism. Hammer falls for three women, including twins (sound familiar, readers of **I, The Jury?**. Stacy Keach was an adequate Hammer but given cliches to speak. The best part of the show was the jazz background score, including "Harlem Nocturne".

I saw ten seconds of Michael Jackson's **Thriller** on cable TV. That was enough. He's enough to give thrillers a bad name.

A pleasant surprise on one of the public TV stations was a 1939 British film, **The Arsenal Stadium Mystery**. Based on Leonard Gribble's very successful mystery, which strangely was never published in the U.S., it is one of the best sports films ever done, with many extended soccer scenes. It stars Leslie Banks, a major British actor of the 1930's and 1940's, as Inspector Anthony Slade, Gribble's series character in at least 27 books. Bank's Slade is different from the books wherein he is imaginative, but basically conservative. On screen he is portrayed as foppish, almost effete, with a tendency to change his hat with every change in mood.

Death of a Mystery Writer

1. **Richard Deming** in Glendale, California late in 1983 at age 66. One of the best hard-boiled writers, he was a frequent contributor to **Manhunt** with stories about Clancy Ross and Manville Moon, the one-legged detective. Some issues contained stories by Deming under his own name and his pseudonym, Max Franklin. he wrote over forty novels, four of which featured Moon. He also wrote ten of the paperback originals in the late 1960's which were published as by Ellery Queen, including two of the best, **Death Spins the Platter** and **Wife or Death**. Deming was a Director of the Southern California Chapter of MWA, and his friends there have established a shelf of mysteries in the Glendale Public Library dedicated to his name.

2. **Leonard Wibberly** in Southern California late in 1983 at age 68. As Leonard Holton he wrote eleven mystery novels about a Southern California priest-detective, Father Joseph Bredder. One novel, **A Touch of Jonah** (1968) is about a boat race from Hawaii to Los Angeles, reflecting the author's love of the sea. He was best known for **The Mouse That Roared**, written under his own name, especially due to the hilarious film version with Peter Sellers.

3. **George Harmon Coxe** on January 30, 1984 in Hilton Head, South Carolina at age 82. He had been one of the last of the popular pulp writers of the 1930's who was still alive. Besides hundreds of short stories and novelets, Coxe wrote 65 novels. One of his series characters, "Flash" Casey, a Boston newspaper photographer, had been extremely popular in **Black Mask** and later appeared in six books. **Casey, Crime Photographer** became a popular radio and television series, with Coxe writing many scripts for the former. Coxe's other famous series character, Kent Murdock, was also a Boston news photographer. He appeared in more than twenty novels.

REEL MURDERS
MOVIE REVIEWS
by Walter Albert

"Houses That Go Bump in the Night"

In French classical tragedy, a major "don't" is the intrusion of the supernatural. One of classical tragedy's less elevated offspring, the puzzle detective story, has kept to that tradition and it has always seemed to me that readers of detective fiction, in general, abhor a mixture of the "real" and the ghostly.

However, I must confess that I am perhaps inordinately fond of a dash of the supernatural in a film or tale of detection and/or mystery. I don't require that the spooks be dispelled by a rational explanation and I'm happy even if the threat is fake spookery as long as it keeps me in a state of shivery suspense for an hour or so. One of my favorite varieties of this kind of fiction/film is that of the menacing house in the country where a faceless (i. e. masked) horror keeps popping out of secret passageways and stretching out a fearsome claw from a panel over the heroine's bed. I think I can trace my affinity to two sources: the thirties serials **The Green Archer** and **The Iron Claw** and a delightfully wacky 1939 version of the archetypical example of the genre, **The Cat and the Canary**, starring Bob Hope and Paulette Goddard. Forty some years later, I remember with unabated delight the scary confrontation of hero and villain in a cobweb-bedecked passage. I haven't seen it since then and perhaps it is just as well. I might be disappointed and, at my age, such disappointments can provide graceless coups de grace to pleasurable childhood memories.

I did see, on television, the 1981 version directed by Radley Metzger. The cast was decent (Wendy Hiller, Edward Fox, Wilfrid Hyde-White and Honor Blackman, among others) but the spooky old house was clean as a whistle and no spider ever survived long enough on that pristine set to spin an atmospheric web or two in a dark corner (of which there were also depressingly few to be glimpsed). Atmosphere is crucial in this kind of film and the scrubbed-up, glossy technicolor versions just won't do. (I might add that I have never seen the highly regarded silent version directed by Paul Leni and am glad to know that this particular pleasure lies in wait for me.)

One of the most phenomenally successful versions of the mad killer roaming about in a gothic mansion on a stormy night is the Mary Roberts Rinehart/Avery Hopwood play **The Bat**. I don't recall any version of that turning up at a Saturday afternoon matinee in my nonage, but I know of at least two film versions that precede my first matinee at the Bijou, a 1926 silent version, and a 1930 sound version, retitled **The Bat Whispers.** At an early stage in my mystery reading addiction, I was a great fan of Rinehart (especially of the delightful spunky spinster series featuring Miss Letitia Carberry) but I did not then encounter an errant bat.

However, on a recent evening i turned out with a number of other "Friends of the Library" for a Mary Roberts Rinehart evening in the University of Pittsburgh's Hillman Library, of which an announced feature was to be a showing of an unidentified film version of **The Bat.** A call to the program coordinator would probably have cleared up the mystery, but I preferred to be kept in suspense, hoping against hope that it would be one of the early versions. My wife and I arrived in time to tour the collection of manuscripts, books, correspondence and other items on display from the library's extensive Rinehart Archives, and I was delighted to find on display (but attracting no interest from the other friends) a number of original Howard Chandler Christy oils illustrating some of Rinehart's early stories. They all featured dashing gentlemen in evening dress in close proximity to handsome ladies with elaborate hair-dos and evening dresses that swept to the floor, all rendered in atmospheric browns and yellows, with only an occasional luminous, bloody red to suggest the criminal stories they had accompanied. This whetted my appetite for an unsettling film and it was with great anticipation that we sat in comfortable armchairs in a conference room improvised as a screening room and waited for the title and credits to flash on the screen.

You have probably anticipated the disappointment that awaited me. The friends of the library and staff are not film buffs and what they had rented for our evening's pleasure was a 1959 version made for ABC-Television, written and directed by Crane Wilbur, and starring Agnes Moorhead and Vincent Price, as spunky spinster and suspicious doctor with a penchant for experimenting on bats.

The dialogue was awful, the budget was obviously minuscule and the movie was shot on a sound-stage with a raging forest fire and exterior view of the country mansion so patently false that there was some laughter from the audience. The saving grace was that, although the setting was rural contemporary, the film was shot in black-and-white. The interior of the "old" house had secret passages and dimly lit corridors that favored the action, and Moorhead was an enormously appealing spinster who, at intervals, gave some hint of the performance she might have delivered with the right materials. The script required that she be both a paragon of independence and a helpless female often trailed by a bevy of younger but not necessarily more attractive women while a series of suspicious male characters were alternately presented as defenders and threats. The last 30 seconds were beautifully handled and this was the conclusion that should have capped a brilliant rendition of the classic narrative. I have not lost my taste for such fare but it will not, I fear, be soon or well satisfied. BLANKSPACE(1 lines) **Post-Script.**

I recently saw a film of uncommon taste and skill on late-night TV, hacked up into short segments that somehow managed to survive the butchering. I suspect that it is in large part because the film, **Mask of Demetrios**, was a kind of pilgrimage with incidents on the path toward salvation/recognition conceived of as short tales integrated within the larger narrative. This 1944 Warner Brothers production, directed by Jean Negulesco, starred Peter Lorre, Sydney Greenstreet, and Zachary Scott, and seldom has a more unlikely combination produced a more satisfying mix. Pauline Kael thought the film was slackly directed and that Lorre was miscast and, surprisingly, made no mention of Greenstreet other than to list him in the cast of actors.

Surprisingly because the film succeeds because of the ease with which Lorre, a writer obsessed with the life and death of the elusive Demetrios, and Greenstreet, an enterprising and shady former associate of Demetrios, following Lorre toward a rendezvous in Paris in gloomy old house with recovery and betrayal, play together. I have not read the Eric Ambler novel on which the film is based and I am not fond of films and novels of international intrigue, but the uncommon intelligence of the script and acting from the Warner Brothers studio crew still haunt me. And please note that there is not a hint of the supernatural in this lingering memory.

Ruth Dudley Edwards. **Corridors of Death.** St. Martin's, 1982, 196 pp.

 The corridors of justice, British parliament, have become corridors of death. Just before the start of the Industry and Government Group (IGGY) meeting, Sir Nicholas Clark, Permanent Secretary of the Department of Conservation, is found murdered. His skull has been crushed by a sculpture named "Reconciliation"!.

 A tangle of governmental titles and more than enough motives are finally unraveled by an unlikely pair. Young Robert Amiss, Private Secretary to Clark, is so junior a civil servant that he must wait at the end of a long line for the lavatory and is "too junior to be properly entitled to start a conversation with any of the national figures". (p. 3) Amiss is sensitive to the determined antagonistic behavior of the late Clark and is, of course, well-versed in the complicated personal politics of IGGY. Detective Superintendent James Milton is in charge of the case. He persuades Amiss to cooperate with the investigation by divulging very specialized knowledge; and so the two take stray ends of the tangle to pull and ease toward the solution.

 It is difficult for the reader to keep the politicians and civil servants straight. Partly because these positions are also something of a mystery to Milton, Amiss has most of the ratiocination while Milton is the tough detective collecting facts and trying to catch suspects off guard.

 Character clues are important to the plot. Characterization is not a strength of the book, however. The main character is unquestionably the victim, Sir Nicholas, who really comes alive as it were. Robert Amiss is also well drawn as is one unusual minor character. The others, including the Detective Superintendent, are not terribly interesting. Still, as with Margaret Truman's inside-government stories, this British counterpart is enjoyable if not entirely believeable. (Martha Alderson)

Lucille Kallan. **C.B. Greenfield: Piano Bird.** Random House, 1984, 175 pp., $13.95

 Lucille Kallan's fourth C.B. Greenfield book is a bit of a letdown. Maggie Rome and the irascible Charlie Greenfield are out of their element, as well as out of the rural Sloan's Ford.

 In **Piano Bird**, we find Maggie in Florida, tending to her ailing mother. Naturally a murder occurs and Maggie is able to coerce

Greenfield into coming down to solve the crime so that Maggie will return to Sloan's Ford.

This book does nothing, really, to further the development of Greenfield and Maggie as characters; a mortal sin for a series book. Rather it seems that Kallan is marking time, and very few of us have the time to mark it with her. C.B. Greefield deserves better. (Alan S. Mosier)

Robert B. Parker. **The Widening Gyre.** Delacorte/Lawrence, 1983, $12.95.

Rumor had it over the past year or so that Parker's Spenser novels were improving. Many readers (myself included) had been put off by three or four entries in a row in which the cooking lessons and the hero's less than silent suffering were insufficiently balanced with action and/or detection.

I was pleased to find **Ceremony** much the best in a long time. Then came **The Widening Gyre.** Quite possibly, this is the best Spenser of them all. While one would wish for more action, the chef's impulse to surprise and educate us has been entirely suppressed. The detecting abounds and is very well done indeed.

The situation is that Parker has been hired to help with the security for a senatorial candidate; predictably, the candidate is one that Spenser would be unlikely to vote for. But the man's devotion to his wayward and alcoholic wife strikes a reponsive cord in Spenser, who took the job in the first place in order to get the fears of losing Susan off his mind. The candidate is being blackmailed with a videotape of his wife; Spenser sets out to recover it.

Hawk makes his obligatory brief appearance as Spenser's dark twin (no pun intended—well, maybe there was). Susan seems won back, more or less, by the end, and even if her return isn't 100%, Spenser seems able, at last, to deal with even that.

Parker has been trying (sometimes too self-consciously) to "transcend the form" and write a modern novel of substance in the Mystery pattern since the very beginning. This time, without sacrificing the detective elements, I believe he has succeeded fully for the first time. Though **Ceremony** came close. (R. Jeff Banks)

Robert B. Parker. **Valediction.** Delacorte/Lawrence, 1984, 228 pp., $12.95.

Reading the latest Spenser novel is like attending a college reunion; a once a year opportunity to catch up with old friends.

In **Valediction,** Parker provides his yearly dose of nostalgia with his large cast intact. The villain of the piece lives up to Parker's level of villainy, and Spenser is after all, Spenser.

With this book, Prker details the widening rift betweena hopelessly love-sick Spenser, and a Susan Silverman intent on finding herself somewhere in San Francisco. I suspect that after **The Widening Gyre** and now **Valediction** that there will be "I hate Susan Silverman" bumper stickers on the streets of greater Boston by this writing.

There is action galore. I especially liked the car chase that starts at Somerville's Assembly Square Mall, and concludes in Charlestown. Being from Boston, I had the pleasure of seeing this "reeled" off in my mind's eye as if it were on the screen. (I often wonder if people from other cities get this same feeling when a

mystery is set in their home town by a talented author; Jonathan Valin fans take note!)
Have you noticed that I have refrained from mentioning the plot? With Spenser it is all secondary. Characterization is Parker's forte, and as usual, it makes the plot a minor consideration. Thumbs up with reservations. (Alan S. Mosier)

Ross Thomas. **The Mordida Man.** Berkley, 1983, $2.95.

The Mordida Man is typical of Thomas's work. Every character in the story, except a few minor ones such as the U.S. President whose wheeler-dealer brother is a kidnap victim, is quite a bit more clever than anyone the reader is likely ever to encounter in real life. The situation is typically complex: the kidnap mentioned above being a Libyan reaction to the disappearance of a top international terrorist who is under their sponsorship. That disappearance was brought about by a brilliant American expatriate bank robber's scheme to ransom the terrorist twice--to both Libya and Israel. The Libyans demand the return of their hero "Felix" in return for the release of the "First Brother"; this is impossible because "Felix" was killed early on by his captors.
The title character and nominal hero recieved his nom de guerre from a brief career in delivering brides to officials in countries like Mexico for the return of arrested American youths (with wealthy enough parents to pay the freight). He is selected to engineer the brother's return, and predictably manages it by unpredictably labyrinthine ways.
All the characters are well drawn, but I have long had one cavil against practically everything I've read by Thomas. His heroes, despite some obvious attempts to make them appealing, usually are insufficiently sympathetic for me to care who wins the fascinating contest of wills and wits--or even what happens to the heroes. If you share that' reservation, you may have to overcome it to enjoy this very interesting read. (R. Jeff Banks)

David Carkeet. **Double Negative.** Dial Press. 1980, 256 pp., $11.95.

Carkeet's first mystery novel is a success on several counts, although not on all. As an especially specialized novel, a mystery whose hero is linguist, it has a guaranteed appeal to avid mystery readers.
The language is fun. The novel takes place at the Wabash Institute where the study of baby talk is the focus and where the tots are in danger from more than just being overanalyzed. The study of infant language and of adult dynamics contribute well to the novel. The construction of events is good until the inevitable moments of climax and denouement. A memory jog that reveals all to the protagonist Jeremy Cook is not quite believable. The chase scene and explanation that follow are too pat.
Carkeet was so much carried away by language play that he named the first victim Stiph (!), a whiny scholar Woeps ("weeps"), a man with an objectionable laugh Orffman, an overly curious colleague Aaskhugh, and the watchful Institute head Wach. (Perhaps those are common names in Indiana?) A subplot as well as the "big clue" rest on further puns. This is really a bit much, even for language lovers.
The pace of **Double Negative** is rollicking, and the characters

likable in spite of their cute names. The ending could have been tighter, smoother, but we definitely ought to look forward to another Carkeet. (Martha Alderson)

David Carkeet. **Double Negative.** Dial Press, 1980. Penguin Books, 1983.

An insitute for the study of the development of language in young children is a novel seeting for a murder mystery, but Carkeet obviously know whereof he writes. He does a good job of connecting the research with the solution of the crime. Jeremy Cook, one of the linguistic scholars on the staff, is the narrator. Another of the scholars, Arthus Stiph, is the first victim. Cook is a likable young man, of rather gross habits, who is convinced that no one on the staff save his friend, Woeps, likes him. Who likes whom, and vice versa, turns out to be important. Only gradually do we find that in a morass of people who do not like one another, there really likable characters. The most unlikable of all, naturally, turns out to be the murderer (but we don't really know which is the most unlikable until close to the end). The method of solving the crimes turns on the unusual pre-speech lingual patterns of Woep's small son. Though the book seemed a bit long to me, on the whole I enjoyed it. (Maryell Cleary)

Dennis Sanders and Len Lovallo. **The Agatha Christie Companion: The Complete Guide to Agatha Christie's Life and Work.** Delacorte Press, 1984, $19.95.

The critical works produced about Christie continue unabated. Unlike the Holmes contingent, so far it has been relatively serious evaluation and recording of facts about the author rather than pseudo-literary "proof" of rather unlikely things. but due to the lack of fresh facts or interpretations the Christie criticism tends to be a contest of who can provide the greatest accumulation of detail.

Sanders and Lovallo's **Companion** does an excellent job of assembling most of what was already known and presenting it in one handy volume. It also has the current advantage of being new so it has the most complete information about film, stage, and television adaptations.

The format of the **Companion** makes it easy to use. All the books are evaluated in chronological order. Each book is introduced with a brief summary of what was going on in Christie's life at the time she wrote the book. Then there are quotes of reviews of the book on publication, a plot synopsis (often only up to the time of the first murder), a list of principle characters, publication data (British and American) and notes of any adaptations.

The second section deals with all the plays, films and television productions either written by Christie or adapted from her work. The final section contains numerous lists broken down by detective for her short stories and novels.

One of the best things about the **Companion** is the integration of material from Christie's **Autobiography** and from Max Mallowan's **Memoirs.** Liberal quotes from these are used to describe both Christie's feelings and to bring her personal life into focus with her writing. Also interesting is the appreciable quantity of related background material. For example, there is a history of the Assuan dams and the moving of the temple of Ramses II contained in the chapter on **Death on the Nile.** We're also given the full lyrics of both the American and

British songs that inspired **And Then There Were None**. These tidbits are informative but not intrusive.

As with any major reference work there are some things to quibble about. There is only minor comment on the various television productions. It would have been nice to know how these came about in view of Christie's well-known aversion to having her works adapted. There also seems to be repetition in trying to make each chapter stand as an individual section. Yet the references to other sections are annoying.

All told, the **Companion** is exactly what its title says. It is perfect for public libraries and for fans who don't have most of the previously published material on Christie. (Fred Dueren)

Josh Pachter, ed. **Top Crime**. St. Martin's, $14.95.
Bill Pronzini, Martin Harry Greenberg, Charles G. Waugh, eds. **The Mystery Hall of Fame**. Morrow, $17.95.

Here are a pair of new mystery anthologies that attempt to provide the best from two different standpoints. The Pachter volume asks contemporary writers of short detective stories to select their single best story and tell why. The Pronzini-Greenberg-Waugh collection polls current writers and critics as to the best short mysteries of whatever time. The results in both case are interesting.

Pachter has 24 contributors, ranging from some of the biggest names in the genre (Queen, Simenon, McBain, Symons) to excellent writers somewhat less well-known (Gary Brandner, Florence V. Mayberry). He has managed to get a quotable comment from every contributor but Patricia Highsmith. The results are of high quality without the extreme over-familiarity that is the main risk of a "best" volume. it seems surprising, though, that Stanley Ellin,whom everyone knows for "The Speciality of the House", would still pick that (his first story) as his best when given the opportunity to champion one of his other fine stories. Writers often resent early success (or pretend to). Michael Avallone's "Every Litter Bit Hurts" is indeed his masterpiece, with a chilling conclusion that is every bit as unforgettable as the author thinks it is. Frederic Dannay picked a late short story, "The Adventure of Abraham Lincoln's Clue", to represent Ellery Queen. While it represents some of the common interests of Dannay and Lee--Poe, Lincoln, and stamp collecting—it is far from their best in the short form.

The Mystery Hall of Fame has twenty stories, with over-familiarity more of a problem, albeit an inevitable one. Among the often reprinted: Poe's "The Purloined Letter", Doyle's "The Adventure of the Speckled Band", Chesterton's "The Oracle of the Dog", Jacobs' "The Monkey's Paw", Futrelle's "The Problem of Cell 13", Burke's "The Hands of Mr. ottermole", and Dunsany's "The Two Bottles of Relish". Four writers are represented both here and in the Pachter collection, only one of them (Ellin) by the same story. Hoch, who picked "The Leopold Locked Room" to represent him in Pachter, is here with another Captain Leopold story, the Edgar-winning "The Oblong Room". (This would seem to settle the question of which Hoch series contains his best work.) Queen is represented here by "No Parking"--and again, I have to say this relatively late tale is not their best, though a good bit closer than "Abraham Lincoln". Pronzini, who picked the locked room mystery "Proof of Guilt" for Pachter, is here represented by "Sweet Fever".

Both collections are recommended for their high quality, though the Pachter volume will offer more that is unfamiliar to the experienced reader. (Jon L. Breen)

Max Allan Collins. **True Detective**. St. Martin's, $14.95.
Andrew Bergman. **The Big Kiss-Off of 1944** and **Hollywood and Levine**. Perennial Library, $2.95 each.

  The last fifteen years have probably seen more real people, both historical and contemporary, appear as characters in novels than did the preceding century. Though some may deplore such muddying of fact and fiction, celebrity "guest-star" appearances can be as enjoyable when well done as they can be tiresome when done indifferently.
  Max Allan Collins sets **True Detective** in Chicago of teh early thirties, where honest cop Nate Heller quits the force to go private after becoming involved in a particularly nasty instance of police corruption. In a plot centering on the assassination of Mayor Anton Cermak and coming to a climax at the Chicago World's Fair of 1933, the historical figures outnumber the fictional ones by a considerable number. Among those crossing Heller's path, many of them shown in photographs between chapters, are gangsters Frank Nitti and Al Capone, gangster chaser Eliot Ness, actor George Raft, former Vice-President General Charles Dawes, boxer Barney Ross, and fan-dancer Sally Rand. Since real people often come off much stiffer and less believable than fictional ones in novels, to feature so many in one book seems a distinctly risky enterprise, especially for a writer, born in 1948, who must depend on research in depicting a time and place and cast of characters many living people remember vividly. But Collins meets the challenge. He brings both the setting and the people vividly to life and at least commits no gaffes obvious to the reviewer's father, who knew Chicago in the thirties. But no historical novel, however scrupulously researched, completely avoids anachronism. There's a reference here to Seabiscuit, who was foaled in 1933 and did not become a famous racehorse until several years after the events of the story.
  Author Collins is a genuine pro, whose years of writing paperback originals have prepared him well for this ambitious and very impressive novel. He has also been scriptwriter for the Dick Tracy comic strip since 1977.
  Andrew Bergman's two novels about the forties private eye JAck LeVine, originally published in hardcover editions in 1974 and 1975 and now available in paperback reprints, did the show-biz nostalgia mystery about as well as it can be done. Though similar in approach to Stuart Kaminsky's Hollywood mysteries about Toby Peters, they are **vastly** superior. In **The Big Kiss-off of 1944**, a chorus girl in a wartime musical wants LeVine to get back some satg films with which she is being blackmailed. Of course, the situation proves much more complicated than it first appeared, involving Presidential politics with candidate Thomas E. Dewey in a key role. Period details are effectively chosen, and the climax during a broadcast at New York's Radio City is both funny and exciting. The shamus changes coasts in **Hollywood and LeVine** with Richard M. Nixon and Humphrey Bogart among the more prominent of a large group of real-life characters. Bergman offers some telling satire on the film world, especially in the description of a screenwriter's funeral. (Jon L. Breen)
(The above reviews originally appeared in **Los Angeles Federal Savings Quarterly**, Spring 1984]

Anthony Boucher. **Exeunt Murderers.** Edited by Francis M. Nevins, Jr., and Martin H. Greenberg, with an introduction by Nevins, Southern Illinois University Press, $16.95.

Christianna Brand. **Buffet for Unwelcome Guests.** Edited by Nevins and Greenberg, with an introduction by Robert E. Briney, Southern Illinois University Press, $16.95

Robert Leslie Bellem. **Dan Turner, Hollywood Detective.** Edited and with an introduction by John Wooley, Bowling Green University Popular Press, $16.95 hardback, $7.95 paperback.

In recent years, university presses have published more and more critical, historical, and bibliographic volumes on crime fiction and other fields of popular literature. But 1983 signaled a new and welcome trend: books in the mystery field from these academic publishers that not only make contributions to scholarship but also provide much pure entertainment for the non-academic reader. Specifically, collections of short detective stories of three very different but very worthwhile writers, two of them of special interest to Southern Californians.

Though he began as a novelist in the thirties, Anthony Boucher achieved his greatest fane as a mystery reviewer for the New York **Times** (once a week from mid-1951 until his death in 1968) and as an editor of **The Magazine of fantasy and Science Fiction.** After the publication of his final novels in 1942, his fictional contributions were in the shorter forms. the first collection of his detective shorts leads off with all nine of the stories about Nick Noble, an armchair detective who ordinarily does not budge from his table at the Chula Negra cafe on Skid Row. A former Los Angeles police lieutenant who lost his job when made the scapegoat in a departmental scandal, Nick has become a wino, a pitiful creature who is constantly brushing an imaginary fly away from his nose. Miraculously, though, his mind is still razor-sharp, allowing him to help current L.A.P.D. detectives solve their more bizarre cases. The Noble stories are ingenious puzzles, very much in the vein of Ellery Queen, often employing a characteristic Queenian device, the dying message. (Not coincidentally, most of the Noble cases first appeared in **Ellery Queen's Mystery Magazine.**) In one tale, a murdered librarian writes the cryptic message "QL696.C9" in her last moments. In "Rumor, Inc.", the victim is on the phone with Lt. MacDonald and addresses a "Mr. Patrick" at the time he is shot--but MacDonald finds there are three suspects named Patrick. In "The Punt and the Pass", a professor is killed in an elevator with his university's two football quarterbacks, each of whom accuses the other when the doors open. Most of the Nobles were written and published during World War II and gain added interest in their reflection of the conditions and attitudes of the American homefront, L.A. style. One of the stories, "Death of a Patriarch", appears here for the first time anywhere. Sold to **EQMM** in 1943, it was never published, presumably because it seemed too unfriendly to our Russian allies during the war and not unfriendly enough to our Russian enemies after.

Another series sleuth, Sister Ursula, a nun equivalent of G. K. Chesterton's Father Brown whom Boucher (a devout Catholic) wrote about under his pseudonym H.H. Holmes, appears in two stories, "Coffin Corner" and "The Stripper". The remaining eleven stories do not have the recurring characters but display the same sharp plotting and writing skill as well as reflecting their author's wide range of interests--opera, poker, football, and true crime cases, to name a few.

In the same format as the Boucher volume is the Brand

collection, the first gathering of her short fiction to be published in the United States. Brand, both a deft stylist and a trick-plot artist in the best tradition of the British classical school, offers sixteen stories, some of them featuring her Scotland Yard detective, Inspector Cockrill. Both Southern Illinois volumes include biographical introductions and bibliographic checklists on their authors.

Robert Leslie Bellem, one of the most prolific contributors to the pulp magazines of the thirties and forties, is a less "respectable" figure in the history of detective fiction than either Boucher or Brand, but his slang-filled stories about Hollywood private eye Dan Turner offer unique delights to at least some readers. The best way to decide if Dan Turner is for you is to read a few selected examples of the Bellem prose:

> "In that split second between the cocking of the heater's hammer and triggering of its release I copped a flabbergasted gander at the bozo who was abolishing me." ("Off-Stage Murder")
> "I fished out a gasper, set fire to it." ("Dark Star of Death")
> "...a set of sheer gunmetal nylons italized the taperd symmetry of her stems." ("Homicide Spike")
> "It seemed a giant pair of scissors snipped me loose from consciousness and sent me tumbling end over appetite into a bottomless black pool which gulped me like an oyster." ("Hair of the Dog")
> "Now as I slipped her the brush-off, her blue glims puddled with brine." ("Dump the Jackpot")

If those excerpts don't fill you with awe and amazement, don't bother to eyeball the works of Bellem. Though his plots are surprisingly cogent, his background of Hollywood's "flickering tintype" production knowledgeable, and his reference to Southern California landmarks full of nostalgia for long-time Angelenos, everything else takes a backseat to the highly individual style that once was the subject of an admiring essay by S.J. Perlman. (Jon L. Breen)

Sara Paretsky. **Deadlock**. Dial, 1984, 252pp. $14.95.

Insurance executive Sara Paretsky began her crime-writing career strongly with **Indemnity Only** and shows even greater control of her materials in **Deadlock**, her second mystery novel. Again the hero of the story is Chicago private detective, V.I. Warshawski, who, as executor of her dead cousin's estate and as a private person dissatisfied with the facts recorded about his supposedly accidental death, begins an investigation. Her sleuthing takes her into extreme danger in the world of Great Lakes' shipping, explores a bit of Warshawski's Polish-American heritage, covers not only the waterfront but also a good many other areas of Chicago, and precipitates a relationship that, at least for a time, enriches the lives of both partners.

Sara Paretsky has done her homework well. Both of V.I. Warshawski's cases show a good understanding of the strengths of the hard-boiled subgenre, and they avoid many of its pitfalls. At the same time, these novels break relatively little new ground. Like Sue Garfton, Sara Paretsky is successful at depicting a tough, autonomous, capable, independent female operative who, in keeping with the traditions of the form, is both human and humane, works to keep her emotions in good control, and follows a code of honor which is always demanding, often painfully difficult to abide by. Paretsky is expanding the formula even as she explores it; her goal is worthy, and her work is sound. (Jane S. Bakerman)

Dick Francis. **The Danger**. Putnam, 1984, 248 pp.

It's very rare to be able to say that an author has never disappointed a reader, but that's what a number of fans do say about Dick Francis, and **The Danger** reaffirms the comment. This novel, like all the Francis books, touches upon horse racing, but as in several recent titles, the scheme in this book comes toward the sport in a kind of slanting way. **The Danger's** hero, Andrew Douglas, works for a security agency operating out of London. Kidnap cases (and kidnap prevention) are Douglas' speciality, and, as always in a Francis plot, the professional details are many, fascinating, and accurate. Douglas' knowledge and his level of presenting it to victims and victims' relatives lends not only authenticity but a unique kind of chill even as his obvious human concern and professional competence reassure. This quality becomes especially important during the major confrontation in the novel by establishing necessary validity for Andrew Douglas' behavior during the climax of a stunning, tangled plot.

The action in **The Danger** ranges from Italy to Britain to the USA, and each setting provides a clever scheme, a vividly drawn cast of characters, and a link to the overall pattern which unites a series of seemingly unrelated crimes. Douglas spots the pattern, studies the links between the cases, and becomes a special threat to an almost-master criminal, one Guiseppe, aka Peter. Also important to the plot--and to the romantic subplot--is Alessia Cenci, jockey, kidnap victim, and hero in her own right.

Sound grounding in human psychology, shrewd pacing of the action, and a splendid control of characterization and setting mark **The Danger** as a book to be read and enjoyed by almost every fan. (Jane S. Bakerman)

Amanda Cross. **Sweet Death, Kind Death**. Dutton, 1984, 177 pp., $13.95.

In **Sweet Death, Kind Death**, Kate fansler, the professor-detective creation of Amanda Cross (Carolyn Heilbrun), visits Clare College to investigate the supposed suicide of Patrice Umphelby, an academic who spent her life "in love with death", but whose actual demise strikes some friends and colleagues as unlikely--and unlike her. Though Umphelby has always declared that she would end her life when it became burdensome, some associates believe that suicide in the face of newly developing career possiblities, in the midst of the full powers of her mind and creativity is unbelievable.

Kate Fansler's cover for her investigation is service on Clare College's committee to consider "gender studies", an issue which has divided the faculty and posed a problem for Clare's young, poised, cool, and upwardly mobile female president. President Norton is but one of a widely ranging cast of secondary and minor characters who aid or complicate fansler's investigation, and as usual in a Cross novel, these folk are major sources of interest. The quiet but intense midlife crisis of Reed, Fansler's husband, provides a subplot no less compelling because it is understated. Once again Kate and Reed demonstrate that they can support one another effectively without meddling and with a

minimum of fuss.
Sweet Death, Kind Death offers all the pleasures readers have come to expect from an Amanda Cross novel; it offers entertainment and makes one think. (Jane S. Bakerman)

Jon L. Breen. **The Gathering Place.** Walker, 1984. 168 pp. $12.95.

By profession Jon L. Breen is a college reference librarian, but during the past fifteen years he's found time to make four kinds of contributions to the mystery field: book reviews and critical work, short stories brilliantly parodying other crime writers, "serious" short mysteries and, most recently, detective novels. All four varieties of his writing demonstrate Breen's primary allegiance to the traditions of the Golden Age fo formal deduction, the era of Agatha Christie and John Dickson Carr and Ellery Queen. In his second novel however, he shows that his sympathies go way beyond the confines of a single genre. This man grooves on the bound and printed word. Old books for him are ikons and old bookshops temples. The more credible you find this view, the more you'll like **The Gathering Place**.

A young woman named Rachel Hennings inherits a musty old second-hand bookstore from her Uncle Oscar and moves from Arizona to Los Angeles to take it over. Soon she discovers that along with the shop she's inherited an uncanny skill at duplicating dead writers' autographs and thereby, if she chooses to use the power, vastly increasing the value of stock on her shelves. teaming up with the book page editor of a local paper and a handsome Chicano police detective, Rachel tries to solve a murder in her store and its connection with the ghost-writing scandal in the background of a best-selling novelist. It's a neat plot played out by a likable cast, including some remarkably friendly spirits who hover around the bookshop like guardian angels, and the result is a pleasurable evening indeed not only for book nuts but for anyone who loves the soft-spoken leisurely type of mystery novel. (Francis M. Nevins, Jr.)

Donald E. Westlake. **Levine.** Mysterious Press, 1984. 182 pp. $14.95

Twenty-five years ago a young man named Donald Westlake quit his job as a manuscript reader at the Scott Meredith Literary Agency and buckled down to the task of making it as a professional writer. During 1959 he turned out more than half a million published words, including the first Levine story. Now that he's recognized as one of the most successful, prolific and compulsively readable of American mystery writers, all six of Levine's cases—five written in the late Fifties and early Sixties and the last about a year ago—are brought together as a collection.

Detective Abraham Levine of Brooklyn's 43rd Precinct would not have been out of place among the urban humanistic cops of the most populat TV police series of his time, **The Naked City**. he's short. dumpy, 53 years old and—thanks to a heart condition that may kill him at any moment--acutely aware of his own mortality, and full of rage at anyone who takes a casual attitude towards death. Each story about him is built around his character and written in an intense documentarian style that vividly captures the Brooklyn, Greenwich Village and Long Island settings and subtly evokes the visual style of the best **Naked City** episodes. Two of the six—"Come Back, Come Back" in which Levine tries desperately to talk a potential suicide off a ledge, and "The Death of a Bum" in which he's the only one in the world who cares about the murder of a petty hoodlum—work particularly well in terms of the protaganist's personality. These however, are the exceptions, and the other tales go off the tracks all too often.

When one reads these stories in succession, Levine comes across not as a genuine character, but rather as a figure assembled out of bits and pieces that are far from consistent with each other. For example, it's only in the fourth story, "The Sound of Murder", that we learn that Levine has a wife and that he's a chain-smoker frantically trying to kick the habit; neither the woman nor the addiction are as much as mentioned in any earlier or later story. Even more disturbing are Levine's occasional bursts of psychotic ruthlessness: in "The Best-Friend Murder" he allows a man to go to the electric chair who committed no crime at all but simply in Levine's view doesn't value life highly enough, and in "The Sound of Murder" he forces a 10-year-old girl into committing suicide with not the slightest qualm. One might be safer with Dirty harry or one of Joseph Wambaugh's street monsters than in the hands of this life-affirming humanist.

The final story, "After I'm Gone", is set in the early 1960s but its recent origin is betrayed by all sorts of anachronisms including a post-**Godfather** Mafia plot, a chain of instant photocopy shops that figure in the events, and the use of slang like "off" as a verb meaning to kill. Its climax however is totally in line with both the original concept of Levine's character and the **Naked City** ambience that runs all through the stories. On the whole Westlake's first attempt at a series character was far from a blazing success, but it was a good practice run and should not be missed by his many fans. (Francis M. Nevins, Jr.)

Peter Dickinson. **The Last Houseparty**. Pantheon. $2.95.

Make a big supposition--you clip a little of **Point-Counterpoint**, **The Great Impersonation**, "Little Louise Roque", "The Sandman", mix them all together into the Clivenden Set, and come out with a convincing, highly original mystery novel. An impossiblity? Well, Peter Dickinson has brought it off--almost.

The Last Houseparty is an unusual enough mystery that I cannot say much without breaking the author's open secrecy. Let me stick to externals. The setting is a stately home on the Thames, just before World War II, where dabblers in the shady side of international politics and the aristocracy of wealth play footsy. At the houseparty there are British fascists who are sympathetic to Germany (but not, they claim, to Hitler), and will do almost anything to keep Britain disarmed and neutral. There are Zionists and an Arab princeling who are very realistic about what is likely to happen to Palestine. And there is sexuality of various odd sorts.

There is a love affair and a hate affair going on. There is a blathering professor who might have strayed out of Evelyn Waugh or the early Huxley. And, most of all, there are two young men, Harry and Vincent. Harry would like to go into politics. The right-wingers at the party will pay his way, but want his political soul in exchange. Vincent is a young soldier with very high mechanical ability. And there is also the wonderful turret clock, with the best train of performing jacks outside Germany. It operates literally and symbolically in the story.

Then things happen at the houseparty. What they were, what

they meant, and what their repercusions are in the 1980's are the mysteries in **The Last Houseparty**, and it is for Peter Dickinson, not me, to tell about them.

This is the best of Dickinson's novels that I have read, a very ingenious idea with complex side issues neatly tied up; the usual good, original background; and beautiful writing. But I did say "almost" up above. I have two reservations. Dickinson is not able to make his central character convincing, perhaps because he (Dickinson) is caught in a developmental dilemma, and perhaps because he ignores legal matters. And Dickinson is sometimes carried away by his fluent virtuosity. But stick with the book beyond the sag in Chapter Two, and you will be rewarded. (A minus, B plus). (E. F. Bleiler)

Anne Morice. **Murder Post-dated**. St. Martin's, 1984.

Tessa Crichton's latest case has nothing to do with her acting career. It revolves around the disappearance (and eventual murder) of Rosamund McGarth, a vague relation of the future in-laws of Marc Carrington. At the same time there's an accidental death when a fire breaks out in an invalid's bedroom. Naturally the two events are finally brought together and the whole thing is resolved by continuous gossip and chit-chat.

Paradoxically, the various characters (and there are many) are interesting, but never alive or memorable. Perhaps this is because the novel is almost totally written in dialogue with scant narrative or descriptive connecting passages. the reader is thrown into the middle of a conversation with each new chapter and must work out the scene for himself.

There is a cozy, unthreatening atmosphere, with almost all action taking place offstage, and then discussed later. Morice seems to be continuing on the reputation built by her first books. **Murder Post-Dated** is acceptable and would be most enjoyed by those who read any mystery they can get their hands on. Tessa is an enjoyable friend who is always nice to visit, but I wouldn't want to live there. (Fred Dueren)

Christianna Brand. **Green for Danger**. Bodley Head, 1945.

This is a superb whodunit set in a casualty hospital during wartime Britain. A patient is murdered on the operating table and a member of the staff who saw something dies shortly after. Even more intriguing; the murderer is known to be one of a small group of people, clearly identified. Devious but fair plotting, super dialogue, characters who come alive, and in Inspector Cockrill, that sharp little man, as good an invention as you'll encounter anywhere. What more could you ask for? If not already tried, Melinda Reynolds should do so post haste--and **Suddenly at his Residence**, **Death of Jezebel**, **Cat and Mouse**, etc., etc. (R.C.S. Adey)

Lawrence Block. **Burglars Can't Be Choosers**. Pocket Books, 1983.

New **Burglar** books are always a treat; those of us who lack a local library attuned to the finer things of mystery life mostly have to wait until the paperback. in this case, it is a book that originally appeared in 1977 in hardcover.

Bernie is his irrepressible self. The complications and climaxes are as ingenious and effective as anything else in the series (and that's high praise). The mystery this time, begiining with Bernie's meeting both the police and a murder victim (presumed to be his) in an apartment he's burgling, is even richer than usual. The puzzles: who was the man who hired Bernie to do a burglary to order, and who was behind him with the money? What happened to the object Benie had been sent to steal? What (or how much) is Bernie's new girlfriend involved in the whole thing? All of these overlap and are frequently obscured by the shadow of the perennial mystery question, Who Dunnit?.

In the course of the story, Bernie ruins his relationship with his "friendly" cop, Ray Kirschman; loses his cover of respectability in his apartment building (and who burgled his apartment?); spends the last bit of his savings on trying to solve the murder; and has greater tests of his self-confidence than usual. But, naturally enough, all is well by the end.

The big mystery is solved by one of those intuitive flashes that mystery readers love so much when we've been properly prepared for it--or at least Block's skillful presentation of that particular denouement makes it seem so. Some of the other unravelling has come before that, and even a couple of puzzle solutions are saved for afterwards. Despite the necessity of an uncommon amount of explaining, the story never drags. (R. Jeff Banks)

The Documents In the Case (Letters)

From E.F. Bleiler, New Jersey:
    First a correction. In my letter on Baroness Orczy and the Old Man in the Corner, I referred to Mary Burton. A slip of the platen I should have caught. Polly is what it should have been.
    For Mr. Deeck's information, the Dover edition of **The Old Man in the Corner** contains the following stories: "The Fenchurch Street Mystery", "The Mysterious Death on the Underground Railway", "The Dublin Mystery", "The Glasgow Mystery", "The Liverpool Mystery", "The Case of Miss Elliott", "The Lisson Grove Mystery", "The Tragedy in Dartmoor Terrace", "The Tremarn Case", "The Murder of Miss Pebmarsh", and "The Affair at the Novelty Theatre".
    The original plan was to offset the magazine appearances, illustrations and all, as had been done with the Arthur Morrison collection. The book was also originally to be titled **The Best "Old Man in the Corner" Stories**, to fit in with the other books in the series. But powers unknown and unseen changed all this. The texts, though, remain those of the periodicals, not the books publications. (So far as I know, though, the two are identical, except for occasional retitling.)
    I'm sorry that Mr. Mogensen is so annoyed with my review. I still think it was fair. After all, I was reviewing a book, and it was my job to point out both sides. I was not writing publicity or fanbackpat. I would like to write only laudatory reviews, for as EFB the occasional writer and fan I know how criticism hurts. But there is also EFB the occasional book reviewer, a hard-hearted, sarcastic son of a bitch who is obsessive about calling spades spades. So, reviews, like that of **Kavalkade**, often turn out as compromises.
    Points. 1. Apologies for having overlooked or forgotten the second Rendell passage. It doesn't change my overall opinion. 2. A comparison between **Kavalkade** and **The Murder Book** is inevitable, the overlap is so great, and others are going to make the same comparison. Mr. Mogensen as author sees the differences; I as reader see the the similarities. 3. Perhaps the term "coffee-table book" has a different meaning to Mr. Mogensen than it does to me. It is not offensive. It is a standard term in American publishing for a type of book, with no implication of bad quality. It is legitimate, though as I said, I do not happen to like the approach, just as I don't like sports fiction, hard rock, or watermelon. To be fair, I mentioned my bias, so that a reader could take it into account. Actually, I had doubts about reviewing the book. If **Kavalkade** had been in a more accessible language I would have left it to someone more sympathetic to both the approach and the authors' interests.

Let me end by saying that I don't follow Mr. Mogensen's comments about the Danish origin of the book. That was never a consideration, and never should be. I have the highest respect for Danish bookmaking, and I don't see why he is raising the flag.

From Michael J. Tolley, South Australia:
Thank you for publishing my letter on Dorothy Sayers in the Jan-Feb issue. There are a few typos in the letter as published for which I do not so much blame you as commiserate: using a new word-processor in a hurry is a sufficient excuse. **(Would that it were!sas)** However, I would like to be exonerated from having seemed to write nonsense on page 45 of the issue, where line 2 of the letter's fourth paragraph should read: "truth without words: they have tongues but are supposed, ignorantly, to" [be dumb].

I hope that American readers will not misunderstand the allusion to Harry Gotobed's dropping coke on the church floor!

From Joe R. Christopher, Stephenville, TX:
I received TMF Jan-Feb 84 this week and there are several impressive things in it. Particularly I was impressed by Michael J. Tolley's letter in response to my Sayers article. I haven't seen any criticism tying her novel to the Elizabethan and Jacobean novellas he mentions, and almost all of his other points seem new also. (A few about the flood in his last paragraph I remember seeing before.) It's a very good letter--I only wish he'd made it an article--and I'm going to xerox it and send it to the Wade Collection at Wheaton College, Wheaton, Illinois (the best Sayers collection in the U.S. for detective fiction mss.). Maybe the curator there will be able to file it so other critics can use it.

I was also impressed by how quickly my "Can We Reach Agreement?" got into print; I know it's because it happened to fit a hole precisely, but nevertheless, it's nice. Since it's a fairly light-weight piece, maybe I should explain what I'm up to. I was delighted recently by the response to my **Q.B.I.: Queen's Books Investigated** (self published--via typewriter and Xerox--not for sale and OP), and so I decided I'd do another detective fiction chapbook in five or ten years. I make long-range plans.) I remembered a paragraph note I published in TAD some years ago about a fouled-up image in a Ngaio Marsh novel, so I thought I'd write a series of fairly short items and collect them as **The English Murder Mystery**. (It's American English in the case of Emma Lathen.) I don't know if I can keep them from being repetitious in form or not, or if my interest will stick with the project, but maybe.... Anyway, that's the game. And certainly there are enough errors in English around. (Maybe I'll vary it with some words of praise.) Most will be shorter than the Lathen piece, so perhaps I'll stick them at the end of some articles--if they're interesting enough for you to continue publishing, of course. **(No question about that.sas)**

I found Jon Breen's two reviews of trial novels--by Cooper and Underwood--intriguing because I think I read a publisher's blurb which said he was preparing an annotated bibliography of trial fiction. Are these part of the project? **(Jon?)**

What particularly interested me in Mike Nevin's review of the volume of John Dickson Carr radio plays was the quotation from Dorothy L. Sayers. Can he give the full citation for the review in the London **Times**? (I realize he is quoting from Douglas G. Greene's introduction to the Carr volume, but Greene gives no source.) I have checked Colleen B. Gilbert's **A Bibliography of the Works of Dorothy L. Sayers**, and she does not list it in 1932—she lists no reviews by Sayers until the next year. I checked **The Official Index to the Times** for 1932, but the only reference to a J.D. Carr which I found has to do with a will (not the right Carr, in other words). On the other hand, Sayers reviewed the following Carr volumes for **The Sunday Times** (a different paper): **The Mad Hatter Mystery**, 24 September 1933; **The Eight of Swords**, 25 March 1934; **The Blind Barber**, 11 November 1934; and **Death Watch**, 31 March 1935. I haven't seen these, so I don't know if they contain the quotation.

It's at moments like these that I wish Guy Townsend still had time to do books for Brownstone Books. I'd suggest that he try to get permission from Sayers' son to collect her mystery reviews. I'd love to have a volume of them. (I've sometimes thought of writing a series of notes on books I'd like to see published in the mystery field, but, as with many things, I never get around to it.) By the way, I have the Carr volume that started me off on Sayers, enjoyed it greatly, and will have my views on it appear in **The Chesterton Review** one of these months.

I appreciated E.F. Bleiler's lists of the Old Man in the Corner stories. One query: in his letter, he lists only the Old Man's last name (Owen), but in his article in **Twentieth Century Crime and Mystery Writers** he also mentions his first name (Bill). What story does that come from?

Wm. F. Deeck will find a list of Roy Vicker's Department of Dead Ends stories in "The Short Stories of Roy Vickers," by Paul McCarthy, **The Poisoned Pen**, 5:1 (July 1982), 3-9. Also on letters: what about Isaac Asimov's **A Whiff of Death** (original and non-Asimov title **The Death Dealers**) for a mystery with chemistry?

Good for Richard Callaghan for sending in his list of the ten mysteries, although I've forgotten (if I ever noticed) what his financial comments signify. I scribbled out a list of my favorite mysteries somewhere, but I lost it before I could send it to you; however, I certainly wasn't going to send money with it or expect any back. I think I've got in the middle of something. For those of us who are absent minded, maybe you should restate the rules on the two listings for letters at the moment...and maybe give give citations of those who have already sent in lists (name, issue, and page). I think it's ten best mysteries and ten best private eyes—with a far earlier request for ten best books of criticism. RealSoonNow. **(I have no idea what this is about and until GMT or someone can enlighten me I can't deal with your request or with Mr. Callaghan's money.sas)**

One final comment: I favor the addresses with letters. **(That's two in favor, so far.sas)**

From Jim Huang, Boston, Mass.:
Guy's review of Cooper-Clark's **Designs of Darkness** overstates—or at least I hope he's overstating—his objections to the book. I'm not familiar with the book, so perhaps I shouldn't try to defend it, but I am hoping that his review's points were more flourish than substance. **(Fat chance.sas)**

A piddling point first: he objects to "name dropping". Though his list is rather terrifying, in the quoted sections Cooper-Clark does say that she's only reflecting the "motion of my mind" (okay, I dislike psychobabble too). Lists aren't necessarily such a bad thing: I find it

interesting that a lit'rary type would rank the form of the detective story right up there with the sonnet and so forth. Too many people diminish the detective story as formula fiction; if that's their objection, then why do they appreciate the sonnet?
The essence of the point--and my objections to the review in general--is that I think Guy is undervaluing mystery or ghettoizing it. There was something of a similar sentiment in science fiction a few years back, epitomized by Dena Brown's comment "Let's take science fiction out of the classroom and put it back in the gutter where it belongs." Is this what he would do to the mystery story?
He continues by citing Cooper-Clark's thoughts on criticism, as an example of her inability to write clear, straightforward prose. But after the quote, he suggests that it is all "bullshit". I agree about the prose: it's not a model of clarity. But academic prose (like medical prose, legal prose, scientific prose, mystery fanzine prose...) is rarely as good as we'd all like. Condemning Cooper-Clark for this is almost--though, of course, not quite--like condemning Simenon for writing in French. It's her language. More importantly, it's the language of lit'rary types. It will hold their attention. And I don't think it's all "bullshit". Her suggestion that the detective story "would seem archaic and hopelessly minor" is interesting. The lines of speculation which begin from this point are fascinating. Why is the mystery story so popular? Is it this very clear linearity which mainstream fiction does not seem to offer? These are not particularly original questions--but that doesn't make them any less interesting.
As to those "certain practitioners of the mystery writer's art, so long as they have qualities which raise them above the common herd of plebian hacks--among whom, I venture to guess, she would she would number most of the authors you and I would count among the greats in the field": it seems to me that the people she mentions and interviews are a pretty good cross section of mystery writers, plebian and exalted. Chesterton, Chandler, Tey, van Gulik, James, Lovesey, Millar, Macdonald, Rendell, Cross, Francis, etc. are all pretty reasonable mystery writers. I don't think we can fault her taste, even if a couple of my favorites are missing. Are Guy's greats not included here?
As to the questions, well, he's right that they're awfully long and involved. But on the other hand, a recent TAD interview featured this sequence of questions: "Which writers do you think most influenced your work?", "How about current writers who have influenced you?", (a question comparing the interview's subject to Chandler, Hammett and R. MacDonald), "Are there any other writers you feel have influenced your work?, and finally "Any others?" **That's** the interview I almost threw away in disgust. There is some idiocy up with which I will not put (as it were).

From Guy M. Townsend, Madison, Indiana:
In the "Grise Notes" which I appended to 8:1 I stated that I was looking forward, for the first time since I put out the preview issue in 1976, to sitting down and reading an issue of TMF from cover to cover and have it all be fresh to me. Well, I'm still looking forward to that experience, and I may even manage to do it before the summer is out. I've had time to glance at Steve's editorial comments and I've skimmed the letters, but the rest of 8:1 (except for David Grothe's review of **Ross Macdonald**, about which more later) remains unread. I'm not, however going to let that keep me from writing a hasty loc just to let you folks know that I'm still alive and as ornery as ever. **(Was there ever any doubt?sas)**

I was disappointed that Steve decided to do away with addresses in the letters section. I found his explanation for that action no less persuasive today than it was years ago when Al Hubin first used it. I'll be interested to see if anyone else objects to the change. My major quarrel with the no-address policy is that, at least to my mind, it makes the letter writers more remote from their readers. **(I trust, then, that my addition of the city of the letter writer effectively negates that argument?sas)**

I'd like to second all of David Grothe's negative remarks about Bruccoli's **Ross Macdonald** and throw in a couple of rocks of my own.

On the back of the book's dust jacket, John Jakes is quoted as having said (or written) that "many scholars can't write; Matthew Bruccoli can". He then goes on to add that with this book "Dr. Bruccoli again demonstrates that enjoyable scholarship needn't be a contradiction in terms". If this book is typical of Bruccoli's writings, Jakes is wrong on all counts. For one thing, Bruccoli over-uses semi-colons, which is annoying as hell. For another, his writing style is stiff, pretentious, and boring. A few examples from page 31:

> An unusually well-read man, Millar has acknowledged the influence of the Icelandic saga of Gettir the Strong, a tenth century outlaw, on his detective hero ....
>
> The name Archer is also borne by Spade's partner, Miles Archer, but Millar has said that the tribute was unconscious. (Millar was a Sagittarius.) Lew came from Lew Wallace, the author of **Ben-Hur**, because Millar liked the sound of it. The aspirational connotations of the name Archer are appropriate for Millar's detective, who is introduced in a novel titled **The Moving Target**.
>
> Lew Archer provides what Millar has described as a welder's mask or a protective shield between author and material that is too hot to handle. Archer not only tells the story; his investigations cause things to happen and extend the web of causality. But he is not the hero; the novels are not about Archer.
>
> Archer is the voice of the author, but he is also the distancing character Millar has created. Millar might well have said he wasn't Macdonald, exactly, but Macdonald was Millar. The pseudonym provided another layer of insulation between writer and material. if Macdonald is a persona for Millar, then there is a double-play combination: Millar to Macdonald to Archer. This idea is intriguing ....

One other nit. On page 70 one reads: "'I honestly believe that Margaret's the best in the business,' he reiterated." But neither on page 70 nor on the 69 that preceded it does Bruccoli tell us that Millar had expressed that belief before, so how can he Reiterate it here? Surely an English professor, if that is what Bruccoli is, should chose his words with more care.

While I am throwing rocks, let me toss a couple in Jon Breen's direction. I like Jon, and I have always enjoyed and been impressed by his writings, both critical and fictional. What's more, I've said so from time to time in these pages. So I hope that he will forgive me these few carping criticisms about **The Gathering Place**, his latest novel from

Walker ($12.95).

My biggest gripe is the result of a personal prejudice and may not bother anyone else among the many, many thousands of people who I hope will buy and read the book. It is my firmly held personal belief, which I will gleefully argue at great length with anyone and at any time or place other than in these pages, **(That's for sure.sas)** that the so-called psychic or paranormal phenomena are a lot of bunk and that people who promote such claptrap are either charlatans, quacks, or self-deluded innocents.

Which is why I was appalled to discover that Jon had made the utterly ridiculous and totally unsubstantiated phenomenon of ghost writing the central element in his tale. I don't object to ghost stories, or to science fiction stories which incorporate paranormal phenomena, so long as such stories are properly labeled, but I **do** very much object to picking up a mystery--the most logical and rational kind of fiction in existence--and discovering, without having been forewarned, that the author not only merely a temporary suspension of disbelief but a total abandonment of reason. (Though I am not very fond of police procedurals, I did enjoy reading an occasional Ed McBain until the unfortunate that i picked up **Ghost Story**, which is labeled "An 87th Precinct Novel" on the title page, and discovered that the ghosts therein are supposed to be real! Jesus, if we can't find realism in police procedurals, where **can** we find it?)

I honestly don't know if Jon believes that ghost writing--for the existence of which there is slightly less evidence than there is for the existence of the Easter Bunny and the Tooth Fairy--is possible, and it is sometimes difficult to determine which characters, if any, are expressing their author's actual beliefs, but when, on page 151, John has an evidently rational character remark that "nowadays, not believing in ESP is like not believing in electricity," I am inclined to believe that Jon may be a self-deluded innocent, since I don't for a moment think he is either a quack or a charlatan.

In another place--regrettably, I neglected to make a note of the page number--Jon has one of his characters cite the woman in England who claims that Mozart, Beethoven, and other assorted musical greats use her as a conduit for transmitting posthumous masterpieces as proof of the existence of paranormal powers. Is it credible that Jon, himself a preeminent pasticheur, can possibly believe such claims? Tell me you are pulling our legs, Jon, and that your tongue was firmly in your check throughout this novel. Tell me that I have wronged you by assuming even for a moment that your's is one of those "inquiring minds" for which the **National Enquirer** represents journalistic integrity at its finest.

Tell me that, Jon, and I'll try--no promise I'll succeed, you understand, but I'll really try--to forgive you for the ghostly earthquake which you use to bring your tale to a close.

One final quibble. Though it does not appear in my **Webster's Third**--sorry, Mr. Wolfe, but I haven't been able to obtain a Second--I believe that "scam" is a general term for con and not, as Jon uses it on page 36, a synonym for "information".

From Doug Greene, Norfolk, Virginia:

I am grateful to Mike Nevins for his kind review of **The Dead Sleep Lightly**. He was much too generous about **my** contributions to the book, but I certainly agree about the excellence of the Carr scripts he singled out: "The Black Minute", "The Devil's Saint", "The Dragon in the Pool", and the title script. "The Villa of the Damned", which he found "rather weak", is admired by some Carr fans. I like it, but more from its main idea than for its execution. As all readers of Bob Adey's **Locked Room Murders** know, one of the most fascinating gambits in mystery fiction is making a house disappear. Ellery Queen, Jacques Futrelle, and Will Scott wrote variations on this device, and Carr had a flat vanish in his short story "The Crime in Nobody's Room". In "The Villa of the Damned", the building doesn't disappear, but all of its surroundings seem to change from the 20th to the 17th century.

As Mike indicates in his final comment, there is enough material for another collection of Carr scripts (and just as valuable, I should add, would be a Nevins-edited collection of Queen scripts). Sometime this Summer, the Carr agents will be seeking a publisher for a collection called **Speak of the Devil**, with the centerpiece being Carr's 8-part serial about the ghostly manifestations of a young woman hanged for murder. This play has a Regency setting, with swordplay, hot-air ballooning, various dandies and ladies of fashion—and a rational solution to the impossibilities.

I now have xeroxes of all Carr's early stories, not only the material from **The Haverfordian** (listed in the bibliography to **The Door to Doom**, but also his stories published while he was a teenager attending preparatory school. His very first story was a locked-room tale. Also included are one or two more detective stories, some historical romances, ghost stories, boxing stories, comic romps, and a serial combining E.P. Oppenheim with Edwy Searle Brooks (I don't mean that literally; I doubt Carr knew Brooks's work). Many of these stories have typical Carrian atmosphere—though not always in the most effective places. In a few months, I plan to write an article on "John Dickson Carr's Apprentice Years" (or some such title) and submit it to **TAD** or **Clue**.

In addition, I'm currently gathering material for a general history of detective fiction, something I think is needed. Thompson and Haycraft are, of course, still valuable, though weak on the pre-Holmes years. Symons is good on the early material, but he has an axe to grind. Haining's **Mystery** is surprisingly helpful for a coffee-table book, but it is no more than a survey. To do a thorough job, I think a multi-volumed history is needed, the first volume to cover the early period through about 1886. So I'm now busily reading the Newgate Calendar, Victorian triple-deckers, yellowbacks, penny bloods, penny dreadfuls, dime novels, and so on. I'll be grateful for any help **TMF** readers can give me. Such discoveries as Jon Breen's about **The Ways of the Hour** by Fenimore Cooper are of the greatest help. Please write to me at 627 New Hampshire Ave., Norfolk, VA 23508.

Incidentally, one result of my research on the early period will appear in **Poisoned Pen**, probably this Autumn. It's a discussion of when the first lady detective, Mrs. Paschall, first appeared.

From Robert Samoian, Cerritos, California:

I don't think it's valid criticism for Art Scott to call author Ken Darby an "asshole" or letter writers Walter and Jean Shine to refer to Darby as the "Rectum of Rectitude". In fact, these puerile attacks so aroused my interest as to what all the shouting was about, that I went out and purchased a copy of Darby's **The Brownstone House of Nero Wolfe** (as told to Archie Goodwin).

I found the book to be well written, interesting, and full of information for Wolfe-Goodwin fans—for example, there is a bibliography of cases mentioned by Archie but never published (shades of Dr. Watson). There is also a listing of unusual epigrams used by Wolfe. There are many minute facts such as that Wolfe left his house in 33 of the 70 cases in the Wolfe canon—some 47% of the time--especially surprising in light of the great emphasis placed on the supposed rareness of such occurrence.

In a time when there seems to be a plethora of books about Sherlock Holmes, it is refreshing to read one about Nero Wolfe. I do not find it incredible that Wolfe would write in a letter his personal views on forced busing, homosexuals, or crime and the media to Archie, keeping in mind how close the friendship of the genius and his chronicler are. That Wolfe would have strong views concerning these topics is in complete conformity with the character in the books--who certainly has strong views about women, food, dining, the police, automobiles, exercise, travel, the F.B.I, you name it.

I hope reviews in the future will deal with the contents of a book, and there will not be attempts to discredit a book by calling its author names.

A NEW *line of*
old-fashioned mysteries

#1 DEATH SPIRAL* $6.95
MURDER AT THE OLYMPICS

ISBN 0-9602676-1-1

PERSE**EVER**RANCE PRESS

Box 384
Menlo Park,
CA 94026

*& more
to come
in 1985

Send for free information

www.ingramcontent.com/pod-product-compliance
Lightning Source LLC
Chambersburg PA
CBHW031435040426
42444CB00006B/821